3 1994 01550 3524

SANTA   RY

'MAY 1 5 2

D0435293

CRAZY TOTALLY AWESOME FACTS

little bee books

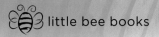

little bee books

An imprint of Bonnier Publishing Group
853 Broadway, New York, New York 10003
Copyright © 2015 by Igloo Books Ltd
This little bee books edition, 2016.
All rights reserved, including the right of
reproduction in whole or in part in any form.
LITTLE BEE BOOKS is a trademark of
Bonnier Publishing Group, and
associated colophon is a trademark of
Bonnier Publishing Group.

Manufactured in China LEO002 0116
First Edition 2 4 6 8 10 9 7 5 3 1
Library of Congress Cataloging-in-
Publication Data is available upon request.
ISBN 978-1-4998-0211-5

littlebeebooks.com
bonnierpublishing.com

CRAZY
TOTALLY
AWESOME
FACTS

J 031.02 CRA
Crazy totally awesome
facts

$14.99
CENTRAL   31994015503524

CONTENTS

NATURAL WORLD

The natural world is all around us. It's everything from the view through the window to beautiful rainforest animals to the fish at the bottom of the ocean. From the largest to the smallest, the cutest to the ugliest, everything is part of the complex web of nature.

THE LAND OF GIANTS

The giraffe is the tallest animal in the world and has long legs and a very long neck. In order to get close to water on the ground, a giraffe has to spread out its knobbly-kneed legs to the side to accommodate its extremely long neck.

The largest lizard in the world is the Komodo dragon. These fearsome predators can grow up to 10 ft. long and have armored scales for protection.

The green anaconda is the largest snake in the world, growing up to 30 ft. long and weighing over 500 lb. It lives in the Amazon rainforest and can overpower many of the ferocious animals that are found there, such as jaguars, caimans, wild pigs, and even humans!

The arapaima is the largest fish in the Amazon River. A fully grown arapaima can grow to about 15 ft., which is nearly as large as their fellow river predators, the black caimans.

The Siberian tiger is the world's biggest cat. It is a deadly hunter and can eat over 60 lb. of meat in one meal!

The blue whale is known as the giant of the ocean. It is the largest mammal on Earth. An adult blue whale can weigh about 180 tons! It is larger than any known dinosaur and is as long as two school buses parked end to end. Also, its huge tongue weighs about the same as an adult elephant!

The largest cactus in the world is the saguaro. Found in the Sonoran Desert in Arizona as well as parts of Mexico and California, these prickly giants can grow to over 70 ft. tall and live for more than 150 years. Once a saguaro dies, its woody ribs can be used to build fences, roofs, and furniture!

The Goliath beetle is about the size of your fist! It is one of the heaviest insects on Earth and weighs about the same as an apple.

Rafflesia arnoldii, commonly known as the corpse flower, is a parasitic plant that has the largest flower and largest bloom in the world. Found in the rainforests of Indonesia, it grows up to 3 ft. across and weighs up to 5 lb. However, it's not great in a bouquet because it smells of rotting flesh!

The fruits of the coco de mer palm tree can weigh up to 66 lb. They also contain the biggest seeds in the world.

Coast redwood trees can reach a height of 380 ft. They are found growing along the Pacific coast of North America. The world's tallest living redwood tree is called "Hyperion," and is 379.3 ft. tall!

MONKEYING AROUND

Apes and monkeys are mammals. Mammals give birth to live young, rather than laying eggs, and feed their young on milk. Monkeys have tails, but apes do not. Apes are humans' closest relatives in the animal kingdom.

Chimpanzees are very intelligent apes. They can "talk" to each other by making sounds and pulling faces. They usually walk on all fours, but they can also stand up and shuffle along on two legs.

Bonobos are dwarf chimpanzees and can only be found in the Democratic Republic of Congo in the dense, swampy rainforests of the Congo River basin. The most vocal of the great apes, Bonobos use clever ways to communicate with each other and humans.

Gorillas are the largest of the great apes and are about 6 ft. tall. Scientists have discovered that gorillas can show emotions and display individual personalities.

The orangutan is an ape. It is the largest animal to live mainly in trees. It has a large brain and very strong limbs to hold on tight to branches. It lives in the forests of Borneo and Sumatra in Asia.

Lemurs are relatives of monkeys. They can be found on the island of Madagascar, off the east coast of Africa. They live in trees in family groups and display lots of interesting behaviors, from sounding like a whale to making dance-like movements across the sand.

It is estimated that there are 260 different types of monkeys, and they are separated into two categories. Old World monkeys, including baboons, are more closely related to apes and live in Africa and Asia. New World monkeys, which are generally smaller with flattened faces, inhabit Central America and parts of Mexico.

The mandrill is the largest monkey in the world. It is extremely colorful. The males are identified by bright red and blue markings on their faces and rumps!

Monkeys spend hours every day grooming each other, picking bugs, seeds, and twigs out of their fur. Grooming is a social activity and is used to reinforce bonds within a family or group, as well as build relationships.

Also known as the finger monkey, the pygmy marmoset is the smallest monkey in the world. It is small enough to cling on to an adult human finger. It weighs up to 9 oz. and can grow up to 6.3 in. tall. It really is a tiny monkey!

Thick-coated Japanese macaques live in cold, snow-covered climates for most of the year and are sometimes known as snow monkeys.

Rhesus macaques are known to be mischievous monkeys. They can adapt to many different habitats, particularly in India where they are regarded as sacred and are usually left alone, even while they wreak havoc and steal food!

One of the rarest monkeys in the world is the golden lion tamarin of South America. Tamarins have a "mane" and a long golden tail. They are seriously endangered because their forest home is threatened by deforestation.

SLIMY, SCALY FRIENDS

Frogs and toads are amphibians with smooth skin. Most amphibians can live on land and in the water, where they go to mate and lay their eggs. Reptiles usually live on land. Snakes are reptiles and have scaly skin. They kill their prey either by injecting it with poison or by squeezing it to death.

A glass frog gets its name because of its see-through skin. You can see its internal organs, bones, and muscles. You can even see its heart beating and watch it digest food!

Frogs can see forward, sideways, and upward all at once! They never shut their eyes, even when they are asleep.

Frogs croak by pushing air through their throat. Most have a sac of skin that swells to make the sound louder.

Frogs can jump more than six times their own length in one leap! Some frogs can jump over twenty times their own body length—that is the same as a human jumping about 100 ft.!

A number of ancient cultures around the world, including the ancient Egyptians and Greeks, worshiped snakes. They were believed to represent strength and renewal.

The small, colorful Sonoran coral snake makes a farting sound when threatened instead of hissing or rattling.

Snakes cannot chew their food, so they have to swallow it whole. Their jaws are incredibly flexible, which means they can fit creatures into their mouths that are bigger than their heads!

Snakes have poor eyesight, so they have heat sensors that can pick up movement of nearby prey. Their eyes are protected by a tough, see-through scale.

A snake's jaw has lots of special tendons, muscles, and ligaments, which give it the flexibility to eat large prey, such as pigs, goats, and antelopes.

Don't go near the decapitated head of a dead snake, particularly the cobra, because it can still bite or inject venom up to one and a half hours after death!

The king cobra is the longest of the venomous snakes and can grow up to 18 ft. long. Male cobras are usually larger and thicker than the females. Cobras flare out their "hoods" and give a bone-chilling hiss when startled. Their name comes from the Portuguese *cobra de capello*, which means "hooded snake."

Rattlesnakes have a "rattle" of old scales at the end of their bodies. They shake these scales to produce a warning sound to scare away predators. The rattlesnake can rattle 50 times a second for up to three hours, which is about 520,000 rattles without stopping!

BEAUTIFUL BIRDS

Birds are the only creatures with feathers, but not all birds can fly. Ostriches are the largest birds, but they can only walk or run, while penguins use their wings for swimming. Birds come in a magnificent variety of shapes and sizes, and are often stunningly beautiful.

The colorful hummingbird is the only bird that can fly backwards.

Vultures are intelligent birds with very good eyesight, which allows them to locate their food or prey from really far away. They also have a good sense of smell and can locate hidden prey up to four miles away.

Thrushes are small- to medium-sized birds and include over sixty different species. They are found all over the world and eat worms, insects, berries, and snails.

The ostrich is the world's largest bird, and although it cannot fly, it is a very fast runner. It can reach speeds of about 40 mph!

Blue tits are European songbirds that are related to crows, magpies, and ravens. Even though they are small in size, these sociable birds show high levels of intelligence and are very adaptive.

The common kingfisher, often considered an iconic British bird, can also be found in the African savannah, Europe, and as far as Japan in Asia. About ninety species exist today, and they hunt for fish either by swooping down from a perch or by hovering above the water before diving in.

The black-legged falconet is the smallest carnivorous bird of prey. Found in the forests of Thailand, Malaysia, Singapore, and Indonesia, it has an average length of about 6 in. and weighs around 1.25 oz. It eats moths, butterflies, small birds, and small lizards.

Toucans live in rainforests and spend their time in trees, but they cannot fly very well. They use their huge beaks to pick at fruit from the trees.

The European eagle owl is one of the biggest owls in the world. It is strong enough to attack prey such as hares and ducks with its needle-sharp claws. It has excellent hearing, which means it can detect the slightest sound.

Birds have hollow bones, which make them light, so it is easier for them to fly.

DEADLY DINOSAURS

No one has ever seen a living dinosaur. The last dinosaurs died out about 65 million years ago. However, fossils of their bones, teeth, footprints, and even their poop have been found. With each new discovery, scientists have a good idea of what these creatures were like.

The word dinosaur comes from the Greek language and means "terrible lizard." It was first used in 1842 by English paleontologist Sir Richard Owen.

Velociraptor was a bird-like, meat-eating dinosaur that lived in the late Cretaceous Period, around 73 million years ago. Small and fast, a fully grown Velociraptor could reach up to 6.6 ft. in length, but was only about 1.6 ft. tall.

One of the fastest dinosaurs was the Hypsilophodon. It lived in groups, and it could run away on two legs if it spotted danger.

Troodon was one of the most intelligent dinosaurs. It was a relatively small, bird-like creature with very long legs, and it could grow to about 7 ft. in length.

Stegosaurus is one of the most recognizable dinosaurs. It lived during the late Jurassic Period, about 150 million years ago. It was a herbivore (plant-eater) and had rows of unique bones that developed into plates and spines along its back and tail. The body of Stegosaurus was 500 times bigger than its brain, which is thought to have been the size of a walnut!

During the age of the dinosaurs, flying reptiles called pterosaurs filled the sky. Their wings were made of strong skin joined to a long "finger" on their claws that connected to their body. They were the first animals, after insects, to evolve powered flight—flapping their wings to generate lift and movement.

Plesiosaurs were a group of large marine reptiles found in seas and oceans all over the world. They had long necks and flippers and could swim about as fast as an Olympic swimming champion.

Tyrannosaurus rex was a meat-eating dinosaur that had sharp teeth as long as bananas and jaws strong enough to crush bones. Scientists believe it weighed more than an elephant!

Brachiosaurus was one of the heaviest dinosaurs and weighed about 80 tons, which is about the same as 17 African elephants. Brachiosaurus was about 52 ft. tall and about 85 ft. long. It is also the largest dinosaur skeleton to be mounted in a museum. Berlin's Natural History Museum houses a record-breaking skeleton that is 41 ft. tall.

The first dinosaurs were believed to be small and lightweight. These appeared during the Triassic Period about 250 million years ago. By the end of this period the first crocodiles, turtles, and the earliest mammals had also appeared.

CREEPY-CRAWLIES

About 90 percent of all the animals on Earth are insects and other mini-beasts. All insects have six legs and three parts to their bodies. Spiders have eight legs, and snails have just one squishy foot.

Tarantulas can survive for up to two and a half years without food. Their bodies are big and hairy, but their poison is actually weaker than that of a honeybee.

The brain of a cockroach is in its body, so even if it lost its head, it could survive for days before dying of hunger.

Ants can lift 50–100 times their own weight. They often work together to lift bigger objects. There are more than 20,000 different kinds of ant.

Beetles are one of the most popular pets in Japan and can be bought in many department stores. The strongest creature in the world, relative to size, is the rhinoceros beetle. It can lift 850 times its own weight.

Female mosquitoes can carry a deadly disease called malaria. They pass malaria on to humans when they bite us to suck our blood.

Bees have five eyes. There are three small eyes on the top of a bee's head and two larger ones in front. When they spot a good food source, bees perform a "waggle dance" to show other bees where to find it!

There are about 900,000 species of insects in the world, and their blood is colorless, pale yellow, or green.

Dragonflies are the flies with the largest eyes and sharpest eyesight. Each eye is made up of more than 30,000 separate rod-like units.

Tarantula wasps stun tarantula spiders, then lay a single egg on them. When the egg hatches, the wasp larva feeds on the living spider!

Scorpions are extremely dangerous, and some of their stings can cause death. They have six eyes on average, and some species are able to survive up to a year without food.

SCARY AND SNEAKY

There are some animals that have amazing disguises and super survival techniques. There are other animals that you have to keep far away from. They may be clever, but they can also be deadly. Make sure you know which they are.

Jellyfish can clone themselves to potentially produce hundreds of offspring, but they don't have brains.

Beware of the box jellyfish! Its tentacles can sting a person to death in less than five minutes. They are found off the coast of Australia and are see-through!

Caterpillars eat an enormous amount during a life cycle stage that varies with the species from a few weeks to a year. Some consume 27,000 times their body weight during this metamorphosis.

Millipedes are usually brown to blackish in color. They have two pairs of jointed legs on most body segments and live in moist conditions.

A large mantis, also known as a praying mantis, measures about 4 in. long. The female lays approximately 200 eggs in a large, cocoon-like capsule which protects the eggs from bad weather and potential enemies.

Cuttlefish are the ocean's most intelligent invertebrates (an animal without a backbone). They are colorblind and have eight arms and two long tentacles, which they use for feeding. They have one of the largest brain-to-body size ratios of all the invertebrates.

The blue-ringed octopus is tiny, but its spit is so poisonous, it can stun up to ten people at once. It usually uses its poison to kill crabs.

The most poisonous spiders in the world are Brazilian wandering spiders. They hide in the rainforest by day and come out at night when you cannot see them.

Spiders cannot digest solid foods, so they turn their meal into liquid form before they feed on it.

Leeches are segmented worms with suckers at each end of their body, and they range in length from about 0.4 in. to over 18 in. Leeches suck blood from fish, animals, and humans by attaching themselves to the host using powerful suckers.

Female flower spiders can change their appearance to match the flowers they hide on while they wait for their prey. This is called camouflage.

21

ANIMAL OLYMPICS

The incredible variety of animals on Earth includes many record-breaking creatures. They can run, swim, and fly amazingly fast. They can be hugely strong, too. These are just a few of the creatures that are definitely champions in the animal Olympics.

Mantis shrimps are tiny but pack a powerful punch! They use their club-like appendages to attack prey at the speed of a .22 caliber bullet—faster than the blink of an eye!

Elephants can run up to 15 mph, but they cannot jump.

An elephant can lift almost 660 lb. with its trunk.

Each crocodile's jaw carries twenty-four sharp teeth meant to grasp and crush, not to chew. That's why they swallow stones that grind the food inside their stomachs (the stomach stones also provide stability).

Sea cucumbers can shapeshift by essentially liquefying their bodies to squeeze through small gaps.

An octopus can squeeze through an opening no bigger than the size of its own eyeball.

Bees flap their wings so rapidly that they can build up a positive electrical charge, which helps pollen from the flowers stick to their delicate wings.

A giraffe can clean its own ears with its 21 in. tongue. It can also last longer without water than a camel.

The blue marlin can swim more than ten times faster than an Olympic champion.

Lions roar to scare off other lions that stray into their territory. A lion's roar can be heard up to five miles away.

Alpine ibex are hardy, adaptable mountain goats that thrive in any climate. They are so strong that they can scale almost vertical rocky ledges and walk on walls. They typically live up to 9,800 ft. above sea level.

Grizzly bears are fast creatures and can run up to 40 mph. They are protective animals and will attack human beings or other enemies if they think their young are in danger. Grizzly bears naturally help ecosystems by distributing seeds and nutrients through their scat (poop).

PLANT POWER

We are surrounded by plants. Even if you live in the middle of a big city, there is a plant somewhere near you. Plants make their food from sunlight combined with carbon dioxide in the air in a process called photosynthesis. Their roots take in water and nutrients, and their leaves catch the sunlight. There are hundreds of thousands of different plants in the world.

Chopping onions is not an easy task because during the cutting, a gas is released that can irritate your eyes and produce tears.

The tiniest tree in the world is the dwarf willow, which is about 0.4–2.4 in. in size. It is found in Greenland.

In the Netherlands in the 1600s, tulip bulbs were more valuable than gold.

The skunk cabbage is a huge, foul-smelling North American member of the Arum family. Native to swamps, the odor of the plant is often mistaken for an irate skunk until the huge golden or purplish flowers are seen emerging from the leaves.

Some plants are insect eaters and gain nutrients by eating a variety of small insects and spiders. The Venus flytrap has tiny hairs that detect when insects land on its surface, triggering its snapping jaws.

Giant hogweed is originally from south Russia and can reach over 10 ft. in height. This alien-looking plant is potentially harmful and can cause rashes and other skin irritation when touched.

Bamboo plants grow quickly. Some species can grow almost 3 ft. in just one day.

Lots of plants are used to make medicines. The painkiller aspirin originally came from the bark of the willow tree.

Bristlecone pines are found in the White Mountains of California and are remarkable for their great age. The most ancient of the species is nearly 5,000 years old.

The Himalayan blackberry is a European species of plant that can cover large areas with its thicket-forming growth. Sharp thorns covering the stems extend like sharks' teeth, so beware!

FLOWERS FOREVER

The giant white flower of the Amazon water lily is the size of a soccer ball and turns purple after pollination.

The agave, also known as the century plant, spends many years without growing any flowers, after which it grows one single bloom and dies. This phenomenon is called being monocarpic.

Rose plants are related to apples, raspberries, cherries, peaches, plums, nectarines, pears, and almonds. Roses are used to make jams and jellies and are also brewed for tea. In ancient Egypt, roses were considered sacred flowers, and the Egyptians used them during funerals to form beautiful wreaths.

The lotus was considered a sacred flower by ancient Egyptians. This beautiful flower blooms in rivers and damp wetlands, but may lie dormant for years during times of drought, only to rise again with the return of water.

Inside a flower, male pollen grains are carried to the female parts, often by insects. Seeds develop inside the flower, which can then die away. Before that happens, though, the flowers give us the most amazing show of their beauty. They often have heavenly scents, too.

The smallest flowering plant in the world is thought to be the common watermeal. Its leaves are only 0.04 in. across. It is found in stagnant, slow moving waters worldwide and often used as camouflage cover for fish and amphibians, such as frogs.

Sunflowers are very fast-growing plants, and in the right conditions they can grow up to 13 ft. tall in six months! They turn their heads during the day in response to the movement of the sun across the sky, from east to west.

PECULIAR PLANTS

Most of the plants around us seem quite ordinary, but there are some truly weird plants in the world. Often, they have evolved to survive in the difficult places they inhabit. Some of them just look extreme, but others can do us serious harm.

The silver torch cactus is unusual because it prefers cold climates rather than hot. It is a woolly cactus found in the mountains in South America and can withstand temperatures as low as 14°F.

Puya plants grow in the mountains of South America, and their stalks can be 13 ft. tall. This is taller than two average-sized men. They can take up to 150 years to reach flowering size, but will sadly die soon after their stunning flowers fade.

Cacti are considered to be like water reservoirs, and although their inner liquid is not pure, it is drinkable. Water stored in desert-dwelling cacti has been known to save lives. Also, the trunks of some cacti are used to make a type of Argentinian drum called a bombo.

The Nepenthes plant can trap insects, which are then digested as food. It has a pitcher-shaped stem and the water that gathers within it is known to be enjoyed by monkeys, hence one of the plant's common names, "monkey's cup." Even parched humans looking for refreshment in the tropical heat have been known to drink from the monkey's cup!

Strangler figs are living proof that clever opportunists get along just fine. Several types of figs are called "stranglers" because they grow on host trees, which they slowly choke to death.

The bear's head tooth mushroom has a fruiting body up to 12 in. wide. Its branch-tips have many long white spines, which hang downward. It also has a nutty taste and mild odor.

The tissues of the African bugleweed plants protect them from caterpillars by producing a hormone-like substance that will kill these creatures if eaten.

29

BRILLIANT BODIES

Your body is the most amazing machine ever made! It is so complicated that we still don't know how everything in it works. All the parts of your body work together so you can breathe, move, laugh, eat, sleep, grow, and read this book!

02

HEROIC HUMANS

The human brain can read up to 1,000 words per minute.

Atoms are the basic building blocks of matter that make up everything that exists. A table, a desk, the air, even you are made up of billions of atoms! We have an enormous number of atoms in our body; a human who weighs 150 lb. is made up of approximately seven thousand trillion trillion atoms!

We cannot avoid getting older. We may slow down, but there are some good things about it, too. We catch fewer colds and other bugs because our bodies have had a long time to become resistant to them. We also, hopefully, have more wisdom from having lived longer!

Humans grow fastest between the ages of 0 and 2 years. Then, as children, they grow at a steady rate. At about 12–13 years, a growth spurt starts that lasts for a few years. Girls stop growing at about 16 years old and boys at about 18 years old.

Muscles (or the muscular system) are responsible for the entire movement of the human body. Each muscle is constructed of tissue, blood vessels, tendons, and nerves.

Humans can't run faster than the speediest animals, and we are not the strongest. We cannot fly or breathe underwater. So why are we so brilliant? Mostly, it is our brains that make us so advanced. Using our brains, we have learned how to feed ourselves, build societies, and use the world around us to make our lives better.

Humans are mammals, but instead of our bodies being covered in fur, we have hair. For men, facial hair grows the fastest.

The main bundle of nerves running up into your brain is your spinal cord. Smaller nerves branch off it to the rest of your body.

Red blood cells transport oxygen, and there are about 25 trillion of them in our body at any one moment. In order to maintain this number, about two and a half million new cells need to be produced every second by the bone marrow. This is equivalent to the population of Toronto, Canada, which is currently 2.6 million!

If we stretched out the 300,000,000 capillaries in our lungs end-to-end, the line would extend for about 1,300 miles, about as far as from Seattle to San Diego. A capillary is an extremely small blood vessel through which gases, nutrients, and fluids travel. Our lungs inhale over two million liters of air every day, without even thinking. Their surface area is large enough to cover one side of a tennis court.

On average, women live six to eight years longer than men.

On average, a person produces about 25,000 quarts of saliva in a lifetime, enough to fill two swimming pools.

BRAIN POWER

Yawning helps us take more oxygen into the blood and get rid of more carbon dioxide.

A total lack of sleep is more likely to kill a person than a total lack of food. You cannot survive for more than about ten days without sleep, but you can last a few weeks without food, as long as you have some water to drink.

Neurons multiply very quickly in women during early pregnancy at a rate of 250,000 per minute. Neurons are cells within the nervous system that transmit information to other cells, muscles, or gland cells.

Just like other cells in the body, your brain cells use a form of sugar, called glucose, to help fuel brain activity. The brain produces between ten and twenty-three watts of power when awake. This is enough to power a light bulb!

Most of the energy generated by our body is consumed by our brain for the development of brain cells and fueling nerve impulses. In other words, the brain consumes 20 percent of that energy despite the fact that it only represents 2 percent of the total body weight.

Your brain continues to develop through to your thirties.

The brain is much more active at night than during the day. At nighttime, the brain processes all the activity experienced during the daytime. Scientists think this is why we dream.

Your brain controls your body. It does all your thinking and remembering. It also sends out instructions to different parts of your body so you can move, speak, and feel. It is connected to the rest of your body by a network of nerves. These nerves carry messages between your brain and the rest of your body.

Your brilliant brain is a gray, wrinkled lump that weighs about 3 lb., and about 60 percent of that is fat. This makes the brain the fattiest organ. It has two halves called hemispheres that are joined in the middle. Each part of your brain has its own job to do. The seeing and balance parts are at the back. The thinking and feeling parts are at the front.

There are so many nerve cells in your brain, you would have to count non-stop for more than 3,000 years to count them all!

SENSATIONAL SENSES

We need our senses to tell us all about the world around us. Our five senses are sight, hearing, touch, taste, and smell. Through our sense organs, we take in information that is sent to the brain as signals. The brain works out what the signals mean and tells our body how to act.

Our ears and noses never stop growing, which is why they often look bigger on old people.

Your sense of hearing is dependent upon tiny hairs deep inside your ears. If you lose these hairs, you lose your hearing.

Humans can hear sounds of up to 20 kHz. The greater wax moth can hear sounds of up to 300 kHz! Kilohertz is used to measure frequency, or cycles, per second. One kilohertz is equal to 1,000 hertz.

In Tibet, China, sticking your tongue out at someone is a way of greeting them!

The human tongue has up to 10,000 taste buds.

Touch is the first of the senses to develop in humans and begins about eight weeks into the development of birth.

Your eyes can process 36,000 pieces of information per hour, and they efficiently deliver data for your brain to process so that you can understand it instantly.

People blink 15 times per minute on average. This is because of the lubrication process that occurs in the eyeballs to protect them from dust or other debris.

Smell is the most sensitive sense, and people can remember smells with 65 percent accuracy even after a year, compared with a visual sense recall of 50 percent.

Women generally have stronger senses of smell than men. Pregnant women often have a heightened sense of smell due to the hormonal changes that occur during pregnancy.

A PERFECT SYSTEM

On average, adult humans can hold their breath for up to 30 seconds. However, Stig Severinsen in Denmark currently holds the world record for holding his breath underwater for 22 minutes.

Blood travels around your body through blood vessels. The main ones branch off into a network that becomes smaller and smaller. Altogether, they are about 60,000 miles long, which is over twice the distance around the Earth.

80 PULSE 80 ABP 88/59

Your heart beats around 100,000 times a day, and 36,500,000 times a year. By the time you are 30 years old, it will have beaten more than one billion times.

Blood is the transport system that takes oxygen and food everywhere it needs to go. It also carries carbon dioxide (CO_2) and other waste materials to the lungs, kidneys, and digestive system from where they are efficiently removed. Your heart is the amazing muscle that keeps this system moving all the time!

Some people suffer from an illness called asthma. It makes the muscles in the tubes entering the lungs tight, so less air can get in. A puff of a special medicine from an inhaler makes the muscles relax again, so sufferers can breathe more easily.

The total surface area of an adult human's blood vessels is about 800–1000 m². This is larger than the size of 3 tennis courts!

When you exercise, you breathe more quickly to get more air into your lungs. Your heart pumps faster, too, to get the oxygen to your muscles. The total length of the airways running through the two lungs is 1,500 miles.

Your heart has its own electrical system that causes it to beat, and as long as your heart continues to receive oxygen, it will continue to beat, even if it is separated from the body. A healthy heart is able to pump 2,000 gallons of blood each day.

There are around thirty recognized blood types or blood groups. The most well-known and medically important blood types belong to the ABO group. Blood types are based on the presence or absence of certain substances, called antigens, on red blood cells. Do you know which blood type you are?

39

KEEPING MOVING

Muscles play a critical role in our movement. The masses of tough, elastic tissue will pull our bones and joints with the help of tendons and ligaments, which allows us to do daily physical activities. The movements that the muscles make are ultimately controlled by the brain and the nervous system.

The minimum number of muscles needed to produce a smile is about ten. Frowning is less effort; you only need to use six muscles. Now that's something to frown about.

Our skeleton is what gives us our shape. Adults have 206 bones in their bodies, some big ones and some tiny ones. They have more than 600 muscles attached to them. Together, the muscles and bones work to move us around so we can sit, stand, run, and jump.

Human bones grow continually from birth until our mid 20s. Our skeleton's bone mass is at its maximum density around the age of 30 years old.

Your bones also protect the soft parts of your body inside. Your skull is the bone that protects your brain. Your ribs protect your heart and lungs.

The area of our body with the most bones is the hand and wrist, where there are twenty-seven bones.

The femur is the hardest, most durable bone in the human body, making it very hard to break!

The hyoid is a horseshoe-shaped bone in the throat, situated between the chin and the thyroid cartilage. It's also the only bone in the human body not connected to another bone. The primary role of this bone is to support the weight of the tongue, enabling us to speak.

The places where your bones meet are called joints. Unless you are double-jointed, some joints, such as elbows and knees, can move only in one direction. Others, such as hips, can move around and around.

Did you know our thirty-three vertebrae (formed during birth) will be reduced to twenty-four when we reach adulthood? The nine vertebrae that we lose go to other areas of the body. Four of the vertebrae end up forming the tailbone, while the other five are used to create the back of your pelvis. Vertebrae are small bones with cartilage in between that form the spine or backbone.

We are about 0.4 in. taller in the morning than in the evening. This is because during the day, the area between our bones is squished by activities such as standing and sitting.

The longest bone in the human body is the thigh bone, called the femur.

Did you know we use up to 200 muscles to take one step? That means our muscles do a lot of work, considering our daily average is about 10,000 steps a day.

Your foot has twenty-six bones in it. Some of your toe bones are very small. A quarter of the bones in the human body are found in the feet!

EAT TO GROW

When your tummy rumbles, it is the sound of the muscles in the walls of your stomach and intestines moving in and out. The noise is louder when your stomach is empty.

Food leaves the stomach and enters the small and large intestine. The good parts pass through the walls of the intestines and into your blood. The parts you don't need leave your body as poop!

The stomach is the center of our digestive system. Gastric juices are mixed with food to produce a thick, semi-liquid paste, called chyme.

An adult's stomach holds up to 2 pints of food, and food stays there for 2—3 hours. Your body replaces the lining of your stomach every 3—4 days so that any strong acids do not get digested.

Saliva in our mouths plays a key role in digestion by moistening the food to help with chewing and swallowing. Saliva also contains an enzyme that starts the chemical digestion of starchy foods.

Your body's fuel is air and food. Food gives you energy to keep you going through the day and to grow. Your body is great at breaking down the food you eat to get all the useful materials, called nutrients, out of it. This process is called digestion. It starts as soon as you take a bite of food.

Your liver is the largest glandular organ of the body with nearly 500 important jobs to do. One of those jobs is taking the good stuff from food out of your blood, and sending it on for other parts of the body to use. It weighs around 3.3 lb. and is a reddish-brown color.

Microbes, such as bacteria, are found naturally inside our gut and have a protective barrier effect against other living organisms that enter the body. They help to prevent harmful bacteria from rapidly growing in your stomach.

Your teeth are coated with a layer of enamel. This is the hardest substance in your body. It can be worn away by sugar and other foods if you do not clean your teeth properly.

Teeth begin to form even before birth. Milk teeth, or baby teeth, start to form when a baby is in the womb, but teeth don't begin to show until a child is between six and twelve months old.

The average person spends thirty-eight days brushing their teeth during their lifetime.

WRAP IT UP

The skin is the biggest organ in your body. It is full of nerve endings which send messages to your brain about pressure, pain, heat, and cold. It also protects you against harm from germs, the sun, and the cold.

Your skin is full of tiny holes, called pores. When your body gets too warm, a salty liquid called sweat oozes out of these pores. Sweat takes heat away from your skin to cool you down.

The skin loses about 30,000—40,000 dead skin cells from the surface almost every minute.

Hairs on your skin add an extra layer of protection from the heat and cold. If you are too cold, tiny muscles in your skin pull the hairs upright to reduce heat loss. If you are too hot, the hairs lie flat.

Skin can be pale pink to dark brown. It all depends on how much pigment you have in your skin. The pigment is called melanin. Pale skin lets more sunlight into the skin than dark skin, so the skin burns more easily.

Fingernails are made of keratin, like hair. On average, human fingernails grow by around 0.12 in. per month.

Have you ever wondered why the palms of your hands and the soles of your feet are lighter in color than the rest of your skin? This is because palms secrete higher levels of protein.

The dust in your home is mostly made up of dead skin cells from you and your family. The top layer of your skin flakes off once every four weeks!

A single hair strand can support up to 0.2 lb. in weight. This literally means that your whole head can actually support the weight of two elephants.

The nerve endings in your skin respond to touch. They send messages to your brain, eventually reaching the area that controls movement, so when you're lightly touched or tickled, your body reacts.

Next to bone marrow, hair is the fastest growing tissue in the human body.

Hair is mostly made of dead cells packed with a substance called keratin. The only living part of hair is at its root, under your skin.

We have a built-in defense mechanism in our skin. If the skin is severely damaged, it tries to heal by forming scar tissue. Scar tissue is not the same as normal skin tissue, but it often appears discolored and lacks sweat glands and hair.

REPAIR AND RENEW

The system in your body that protects you from disease is called your immune system. Allergies happen when your immune system decides to attack a substance that is harmless. Some people are allergic to nuts, while others are allergic to dairy products. An allergy to the pollen in plants is called hay fever.

Did you know that even a very painful bruise on our skin can be healed automatically with the help of our immune system? This is because new tissues are formed to replace the dead ones, and the dead blood and tissue cells are carried away by the bloodstream.

The liver is the most resilient organ and is capable of regenerating itself. If only 25 percent is healthy, it can regenerate into a complete liver again!

Jet lag is a feeling of extreme tiredness and confusion after a long flight. It is the result of your body finding it difficult to adjust to a new time zone. The more time zones you cross during a long flight, the more severe the jet lag can become.

Everybody feels ill sometimes. It's not fun, but usually we get better quite quickly! Your body is fantastic at repairing itself. When it comes under attack from germs and other diseases, it goes into battle mode. All systems work together to defeat the enemy and make you better.

Having a good night's sleep is the best way to let your body renew itself. In the morning, you will wake up refreshed and ready for anything! During sleep, the body has a chance to replace chemicals and repair muscles, other tissues, and aging or dead cells.

The brain and nerve cells are the only cells in the body that cannot regenerate. Once brain cells are damaged they cannot be replaced.

We lose hundreds of hairs a day, but you'll have to lose a lot more before you or anyone else will notice. Half of the hairs on your head can disappear before anyone notices they've gone!

Every minute, a healthy young body makes about three hundred million new cells to replace the ones that naturally wear out and die.

As you get older, your hair will change color due to the lack of pigment-forming cells that give your hair color. Initially, hair is white and gets its natural color from this pigment called melanin. The chance of your hair going gray increases 10–20 percent every decade after thirty years.

47

LIFE STORIES

It is more than sixteen years since the new century began in 2000, but some people have seen three centuries in their lifetime! One of them was a Japanese woman who was born in 1898. At 117 years of age, she was the oldest living person, until her death in 2015.

In the UK, when you reach your 100th birthday, you may receive a message of congratulations from the Queen. More than 13,000 people are over 100 years old in the UK today.

The record for the oldest person who ever lived was a French woman called Jeanne Calment. When she died in 1997, she was 122 years and 164 days old. She was still riding a bicycle at the age of 100.

The tallest man ever was Robert Wadlow from the United States. In 1940, he measured 8 ft. 11.1 in. tall! He had the biggest feet ever, too. They were 18.5 in. long.

Ask anyone who has lived a long life, and they will tell you that the secret is to keep active. Many of the world's oldest people are still exercising regularly in their 80s and 90s, even their 100s! They also say that they eat properly and sleep well. Some people have lived long lives, and others have broken records in weird and wonderful ways, using their unique body parts!

Xie Qiuping from China holds the record of having the world's longest hair, measured at 18 ft. long. When asked by the media for the reason why her hair was so long, she explained that she stopped visiting the hair salon more than fifty years ago as she often got sick after a haircut.

Have you heard of the guy who eats McDonald's burgers all the time? His name is Don Gorske, and he comes from Wisconsin. In 2008, he earned a place in the record books for "Most Big Macs consumed," having eaten over 26,000 of them.

Joaquín Balaguer was the oldest president of the Dominican Republic, who left office at the age of 89. He was successfully elected as the president for three terms during the periods 1960–62, 1966–78, and 1986–96.

The longest beard on a living person measured 7 ft. 9 in. in 2010. It belonged to Sarwan Singh of Canada.

The longest fingernails ever measured belonged to Lee Redmond of the United States. In 2008, they grew to 28 ft. 4.6 in.

At 1 ft. 9 in. Chandra Bahadur Dangi, from Nepal, who died in September 2015, was the shortest man in the world.

Former South African President Nelson Mandela lived to be 95 years old. The average life expectancy in South Africa is about 53 years.

DEADLY DISEASES

There are thousands of different diseases that can make us sick. Some are infectious, so we can catch them from other people. Others might be inherited from our parents. Some we catch from organisms in the environment. Luckily, doctors now understand a lot about many diseases, and they can treat people back to good health.

Infectious diseases are mostly caused by two kinds of tiny organisms called viruses and bacteria. They are spread through the air, on animals, or in water.

When one infectious disease affects many people at once across a large area, it is called an epidemic. Flu epidemics can occur every few years, usually in winter.

When an epidemic of a disease spreads to more than one continent and affects millions of people, it is called a pandemic. There were several flu pandemics around the world in the twentieth century. The worst flu pandemic recorded was the so-called Spanish Flu outbreak in 1918, when between 20 and 50 million people died.

The worst pandemic disease, which ravaged Europe during most of the 1300s, was bubonic plague. Characterized by the appearance of oozing and bleeding sores on the body and a high fever, the plague killed about 75 to 200 million people during the 14th century alone, a third of the world's population at the time.

Due to eating habits in the USA, one in three children born in the year 2000 has a chance of getting Type II diabetes.

Food poisoning is an illness caused by eating food contaminated by bacteria. The main symptoms include a bad stomachache leading to nausea, vomiting, and diarrhea. In very extreme cases it can even lead to death.

Malaria is a deadly disease which is transmitted through a mosquito bite. Every year, around 200 million people are diagnosed with the disease. Scientists are in the process of making a vaccine that will be able to protect people against the disease.

Some diseases are not infectious. Cancer is a disease where some cells grow too quickly and form a lump. Scientists are working to develop treatments for these kinds of diseases.

Viruses are usually around one hundred times smaller than bacteria. The ebola virus is particularly dangerous. It causes a very bad fever, and about half of people who catch it die. It originated in Africa.

STOP EBOLA !! NO ENTRANCE WITHOUT PERMISSION

MEDICAL MARVELS

Our understanding of medicine is improving all the time. Scientists and doctors are working hard to find better ways to diagnose diseases, which means figuring out which disease a person has. Once they know that, they can work on the best ways to treat it. The best solution is to prevent diseases from happening in the first place. Medicine is developing all the time to help aid prevention and improve survival rates.

Sometimes, the best way to treat an illness is through surgery. This means opening up the body and repairing or removing the damaged part.

Fewer than one hundred years ago, scientists discovered antibiotics. These drugs can kill the bacteria that cause diseases. Antibiotics have transformed medicine and saved millions of lives.

Antibiotics do not work against infections caused by viruses, such as colds, flu, most sore throats, bronchitis, and many sinus and ear infections.

The World Health Organization (WHO) has the job of looking at international public health. It can create health campaigns and respond when outbreaks happen. World Health Day is on April 7 each year.

Vaccines, usually given as an injection by a needle in your arm or leg, are fluids that help your body to build up a defense and protect against diseases caused by certain germs.

In the past sixty years, vaccines have helped eradicate one disease (smallpox) and are close to eradicating another (polio). Vaccines prevent more than 2.5 million deaths each year.

Regenerative medicine is the process of creating, replacing, or repairing damaged tissue or lost organs due to various causes such as aging or diseases. Scientists grow tissues and organs in an incubator located under laboratory conditions and safely implant them in the patient's body to restore or establish normal function.

There has been a tremendous improvement in the medical field during the last decade. One of the important breakthroughs is stem cell research. A stem cell is capable of becoming a different cell type in the body, such as skin, muscle, or nerve cells. This ability means there is the potential to better treat illnesses that affect us all, and a lot of important research is currently being carried out.

LOUIS PASTEUR
1822-1895
POSTES

Until the late 1800s, people did not even know that germs, called bacteria, were the cause of many diseases. A French scientist named Louis Pasteur figured it out and proved it.

NEW FRONTIERS

Animal insulin was the first type to be administered to humans in order to control diabetes by stabilizing sugar intake. Derived from cows and pigs, the use of animal insulin has now largely been replaced by human insulin, but it is still available on prescription when necessary.

Scottish bacteriologist Sir Alexander Fleming discovered penicillin. He shares the 1945 Nobel Prize for Physiology or Medicine with Ernst Chain and Sir Howard Florey.

Scientists have created many drugs that can cure people of diseases they would have died from in the past. They are always looking for ways to improve old drugs and invent new ones.

Magnetic resonance imaging (MRI) is a radiology technique that can produce clear photos of the body's structure through strong magnetic fields and radio waves. It can be used to examine the brain, heart, blood vessels, spinal cord, bones, joints, and internal organs to accurately detect the presence of disease and damage.

Doctors performed the first full face transplant three years ago, but this type of intricate surgery is still extremely rare. However, the success of this pioneering surgery is likely to mean other similar operations will be carried out in the future.

Thousands of people around the world are working to make medicine even better. Some of them are scientists working in laboratories. Others are doctors and surgeons, who are learning from their patients. Some are nurses and other caretakers, who are looking after the sick. The future for world medicine is certainly bright.

There are more than 3,000 drugs to treat cancer in development around the world.

Our genes are like instructions in our cells that make us what we are. They decide everything about us, including any diseases we may have inherited. Scientists know a lot about the codes in our genes and use that knowledge to find ways to treat diseases.

Heart bypass surgery is a major surgery carried out to treat heart disease when your coronary arteries are blocked, especially when blockages are above 70 percent. Your doctor may treat the problem by giving the blood a new pathway to the heart.

One of the achievements of modern medicine is the computerized tomography (CT) scan. It helps doctors to visualize the heart's anatomy to diagnose heart disease by using X-rays and a computer to create detailed images of inside our bodies.

FASCINATING FOOD

We have to eat to stay alive! These days we can try foods from all around the world, no matter where we live, and there are many exciting flavors and smells to enjoy. Some of the things people like eating can seem a bit odd to others!

03

EAT TO LIVE

The foods you eat make up your diet. A healthy diet contains foods of several different kinds, called food groups. These groups go well together, and they support your body in different ways. You need to eat more foods from some groups than others.

Pork is naturally low in salt and would provide a rich source of protein in your diet, if you are a meat eater. One serving of pork provides you with about half of the protein you need in the day.

Iron is an essential nutrient, and a lack of it in our diets could eventually lead to anemia (low red blood cell count) and other iron-deficiency diseases. Foods rich in iron include dark, leafy vegetables, legumes, beans, fish, egg yolks, and red meat.

Some foods that are good sources of protein are fish, cheese, and eggs. They also contain vitamins and minerals. Nutritious and high in omega-3 fatty acids, eggs are known to help build brain cell membranes.

We need protein in our diet to help build tissues, cells, and muscles. Meat is a good source of protein. Meat is also a good source of vitamins and minerals, such as iron, selenium, and zinc.

Fish is really good for you. It is known as "brain food"! Firm, oil-rich fish such as salmon, tuna, mackerel, and trout are full of healthy omega-3 fats as well as protein. The Japanese eat fish raw, in sushi and sashimi.

To give you energy, you should include some carbohydrates (carbs) in your diet. These foods include bread, pasta, rice, and potatoes. They're all tasty, too!

The average person in a rich country will consume 110 tons of food and 12,000 gallons of water in their lifetime. More than 3.9 trillion gallons of water are consumed in the USA per month.

Fast food, such as hamburgers, is very popular but is not the best choice for you, for animals, or for the planet! For example, every pound of hamburger meat we consume takes 2,500 gallons of water and 16 lb. of grain to produce, as well as the land needed to raise the cattle and the grains to feed them.

In the past, sailors on long voyages could not get ahold of fresh vegetables and fruit to eat, so they did not get enough vitamin C in their diet. This caused a disease called scurvy, which resulted in sailors getting sore limbs and bleeding, swelling gums, leading to their teeth falling out.

GROWING IT

Food is grown all over the world. Some people grow enough food to feed their families, and farmers and food manufacturers grow enough to sell in stores. Growing food to feed the 7.3 billion people in the world is a big task! Modern technology has helped us to develop ways to grow food on a huge scale.

As long as you are not wheat intolerant, a certain amount of wheat in your diet is beneficial. It has a low fat content and is a high source of energy and fiber. It is also known to regulate blood glucose levels in diabetic patients.

Wheat is the world's most widely grown plant. There are huge areas of wheat fields in the United States, and a lot of the wheat grown is used to make bread and pasta. Americans eat 38,581 tons of pasta every year!

Some farmers use their land to rear animals instead of growing crops. Modern cattle farms can be very big and are home to thousands of cows.

Yams, plantains, green bananas, eggplant, and cassava are the essential staples in Africa, where they are grown all over the continent. These vegetables are an excellent source of carbohydrates and vitamin B6. It's important to choose healthy carb options to help boost energy.

More than 7,000 different kinds of apple are grown around the world, but only a handful of these are available to buy.

Soybeans are packed with protein. Grown from seed in widespread areas such as the USA, Brazil, Argentina, China, and India, soybeans are becoming more and more a part of daily diets.

Slash-and-burn is a wasteful way of growing food. Land is burnt to clear it of plants, and then it is used to grow crops. When the soil is no longer fertile, the farmers move on and find new land to clear. Huge areas of the Amazon rainforest in South America have been destroyed in this way.

An important staple food, the potato is very popular and served in many different ways. The United States produces 5.2 percent of the world's total potatoes—that's potentially a lot of fries! UK scientists have recently identified blood pressure-lowering compounds in this vegetable, called kukoamines.

Bananas are widely cultivated in more than 150 countries throughout the tropics and subtropics. A very popular, easy-to-eat fruit, there are about 1,000 varieties.

Organic farming does not use chemical fertilizers on crops or feed additives for livestock. Farmers use seaweed or manure (animal poop!) to grow their crops instead. This costs more money but is better for the environment because natural habitats are less threatened, and the soil is generally enhanced because of the manure used.

FEEDING THE WORLD

Tea and coffee both contain caffeine, but tea doesn't have as much. The antioxidants in tea can help to protect against cardiovascular and degenerative diseases. Next to water, tea is the most widely consumed beverage in the world and can be found in almost 80 percent of all US households. On a typical day, over 158 million Americans are drinking tea!

It is said that coffee was first noticed by shepherds in the highlands of Ethiopia. The goats they were herding appeared to become frisky after eating coffee tree berries and would not easily settle down. Look how many countries enjoy drinking coffee today, thanks to those goats!

Hunger is a devastating but very real experience for some people. In sub-Saharan Africa, more than one in four people remains chronically undernourished, while in Asia, about 526 million people suffer from hunger.

With modern technology, it should be possible to grow enough food to feed all the people in the world. Sadly, the food that we grow doesn't reach some poorer countries. In rich parts of the world, people have access to plenty of food, and many people eat too much! In poor parts of the world, many people do not have enough to eat because they can't afford to grow or buy food.

Recipes from some countries have spread around the world after people have visited those places and enjoyed the food. Food from China and India, for example, is now popular all over the planet.

Idli is a steamed cake made from rice and black lentils, and is most popular in southern India. Doctors have been known to prescribe idli to patients suffering from sickness and fever to help them recover, as they believe it has healing and soothing properties.

Thailand exports around 850,000 tons of rice to Africa per year, of which the majority will go to South Africa. India, Pakistan, and the USA are also big exporters of rice.

Since we have access to food from all over the world, it sometimes has to travel a long way to reach us. Road and rail links are the major transportation routes, and the demand for all the different food products make the delivery process a big business!

Worker bees need to visit 2 million flowers in order to make a 1 lb. jar of honey. That's a lot of flowers! Honey contains nutritional and medicinal properties that have been used since the days of the pharaohs in ancient Egypt.

Rice is low in fat and high in energy. It is a staple food for half the world's population, but mostly in Asia. It is an excellent source of vitamins and minerals such as niacin, vitamin D, calcium, fiber, iron, thiamine, and riboflavin. These vitamins help to maintain a good immune system and generally keep our bodies functioning as efficiently as possible. In India, rice is associated with good fortune and the Hindu goddess of wealth and purity, Lakshmi.

FANTASTIC FRUITS

Fruits are juicy, they are sweet—everyone loves to eat fruit! Fruit is good for us and is an important part of a healthy diet. There are thousands of different fruits grown and eaten around the world. Some are more unusual than others.

Lemons are bright yellow citrus fruits, very high in vitamin C. They originated in southern Asia and later reached the Middle East. The heaviest lemon ever grown was recorded in Israel, weighing 11 lb. 9.7 oz., and it was 13.7 in. tall. California is full of lemon trees.

Apple trees first grew in central Asia before they spread across the world. European explorers took them to the Americas. Today in the United States, thirty-six states grow apples.

The pineapple plant has more than 200 flowers on it, which join together to create one pineapple fruit.

Tomatoes are very popular throughout the world, but did you know that they are a fruit, not a vegetable? Because the tomato contains seeds on the inside, it belongs to the fruit family.

The papaya is a delicious tropical fruit. It is nutritious and fleshy and can even help relieve some digestive and urinary problems.

The durian fruit that grows in Asia really stinks! The smell is so bad that it is banned from many public places. Despite its stinky scent, it's delicious to eat.

As of 2013, the world record for the heaviest watermelon is for one grown by Chris Kent in Tennessee. The watermelon weighed a whopping 350.5 lb! That is equivalent to two average sized adults!

Did you know that grapes will explode if they are put in a microwave? The juiciness of the grape combined with the electromagnetic waves causes a chemical reaction!

There are different varieties of mangoes, and India exports around 17.5 million tons of this popular fruit every year.

Strawberries are not really fruits because their seeds are on the outside. Technically, a fruit contains the plant's seeds on the inside.

Purple mangosteen has to be grown in temperatures of above 40°F. This is as cold as the inside of an average domestic fridge. If it is grown in temperatures below that, the plants will die. The mangosteen fruit is the national fruit of Thailand.

A rainbow of colorful vegetables not only looks enticing on the plate but is also very good for you. Vegetables all contain different and important vitamins that your body needs in order to thrive and grow. Choose those that are the brightest and eat as many shades as possible.

The longest carrot ever grown was in the UK in 2007, and it measured 19 ft. 1.96 in. long! That's huge! It is about the length of a small boat.

Carrots were originally whitish in color. It was thought to be the Dutch carrot growers who first introduced the shade of orange in the seventeenth century in honor of their Royal Family's traditional color.

There are thousands of different kinds of vegetables. Today, we can grow, buy, and eat vegetables from all over the world. Wherever they come from, we need to eat a lot of them to stay healthy.

Baked beans are delicious, and they are healthy, too. They contain a lot of protein and not much fat.

Asparagus is rich in folic acid, and the minerals and amino acids within it can protect the liver against toxins. It can act as a diuretic, which means you may need to urinate more frequently. The disadvantage of this vegetable is that it quickly loses its flavor once it's been cut.

Potato plants are related to a poisonous plant known as deadly nightshade. Both can contain a poison called solanine. Green bits on a potato skin may contain solanine, so be sure to remove them before cooking!

The ancient Romans called onions "large pearls." They were a highly prized vegetable. The ancient Egyptians really loved them, too. They buried them with their kings, or pharaohs, and presented baskets full of them as funeral offerings.

Bell peppers are usually sold green, but they can also be red, purple, or yellow.

Popeye was definitely on to something when consuming all that spinach! Known as one of the superfoods because of its energy boosting properties, spinach is a dark green vegetable, of which the leaves are the only edible part. Thanks to the promoters of this cartoon, spinach consumption increased by 33 percent.

Once a year, on the last Wednesday in August, the tiny Spanish town of Buñol becomes the setting for a huge tomato fight! Known as La Tomatina, thousands of revelers throw tomatoes at each other in celebration of the famous fruit. It gets extremely messy!

Iron-rich vegetables such as the pumpkin take between 85 and 125 days to grow and have about 500 seeds. The pumpkin is very popular during Halloween, when thousands of them are hand-carved into spooky faces and filled with candles. The flowers that grow on pumpkin vines are also edible.

Chili is an important element in Indian foods, as it adds aroma and creates a heat to the taste buds. The hottest known chili is the Carolina Reaper, which is 300 times hotter than a jalapeño!

EATING MEAT

Most people around the world eat meat as part of their diet. In poorer countries, people often eat less meat than people in richer countries. Some people choose not to eat meat at all; they are vegetarians. Vegans choose not to eat any animal products at all!

Beef cattle production is a big business in the United States, and it produces more beef than any other country. Over 2,000 quarter pounders can be made from one average-sized cow!

Pork is the meat most eaten by weight in the world, but goat is the most widely consumed meat worldwide. No kidding!

People in India eat the least amount of meat compared to other countries. This is partly because the main religion practiced there is Hinduism, and Hindus do not eat meat.

More than 50 billion chickens are reared every year as a source food for their meat and eggs. Some of them are reared outdoors, where they are given free range, and others are reared in large compounds.

We eat about 100 million tons of poultry every year.

Insects contain the highest levels of protein and the lowest amounts of fat. Fried grasshoppers are a Mexican delicacy!

Ever considered eating snake?! In China, snake soup is a common dish on the menu, and barbecued snake is pretty popular, too!

Frogs' legs are an important part of French and Cantonese cuisine. Indonesia has become the largest exporter of frogs to Europe.

Some animal farmers are nomadic. This means that they travel around with their herds, looking for fresh grazing land. These nomads live in Mongolia, Asia.

DELICIOUS DAIRY

Foods made from milk are called dairy products. Butter, cheese, and ice cream are all dairy products. They contain calcium, which makes our bones strong. They also contain a lot of fat, so we shouldn't eat too much of them. There are thousands of different cheeses made around the world. It would take a lifetime to try them all!

A lactometer (or galactometer) is an instrument used to measure the relative density of milk, which then determines its quality and purity.

When possible, ice cream was served to soldiers during World War II, despite the strict rationing, in a bid to lift their spirits. The first floating ice cream parlor was built for sailors in the western Pacific in 1945.

Historically, buttermilk was a liquid made by churning butter from cream. It is low in fat, nourishing, and has a unique flavor. In India, buttermilk is known as chaas and is consumed as a cooling drink.

In 1856, French scientist Louis Pasteur discovered that heating milk to a high temperature kills the bacteria in it. This process is called pasteurization, and it protects the purity and taste of the milk we buy.

In 2014 the oldest-known cheese in the world was found buried in the sand with a mummified body, in the Taklamakan Desert in China. It had been there for 3,600 years! The dry conditions preserved the cheese surprisingly well.

Did you know that a single dairy cow can produce 2,537 gallons of milk per year? That's over 20,000 pints!

About one-fifth of all the cheese produced in the United States is used on top of pizzas.

Both nutritious and delicious, milk products provide the right amount of bone-building nutrients, specifically calcium, vitamin D, protein, magnesium, potassium, and zinc. That's a whole lot of goodness!

Gorgonzola is a kind of Italian cheese. It has veins of blue fungus in it. It has been made in northern Italy since the year 879 CE!

In desert countries in the Middle East, people drink the milk of camels. It has more nutrients than cow's milk, and in those countries it is also used to treat some illnesses.

71

WHO EATS THAT?

Different people have different ideas of what tastes good. In some parts of the world, people eat foods that others might think are a bit strange or taste weird! Over the centuries, people have learned to make food from the ingredients available to them.

Monkey brains were once eaten by certain tribal chiefs of Cameroon during their religious customs and festivals.

In Thailand, southeast Asia, people enjoy giant water bugs served with chili and sticky rice. They also like to add dung beetles to their curries!

Shrimp is a popular dish in parts of China. Their still wriggling bodies are soaked in liquor to slow down their movement before they are eaten. This recipe is also popular in parts of the United States.

In Korea, people eat live octopuses!

In China, fermented tofu is a popular street food dish. The stench of stinky tofu is decidedly unpleasant, but when it is well prepared, the taste is surprisingly flavorful.

Buzz off! Wasp crackers actually do contain wasps! Boiled, dried, and infused, the wasps are spread into the cracker, which can be bought in Japan.

In France, there is a tradition of eating exotic meats on Christmas Day. People eat kangaroo, crocodile, and ostrich. Once cooked, ostrich and kangaroo look similar to beef.

The Swedish delicacy, surströmming, is fermented fish. This tinned food smells so awful that the official advice is to open the tin outdoors, but then to eat it indoors because the rotten smell attracts flies.

Commonly eaten in southeast Asian countries such as Cambodia, cooked edible sago grubs are said to taste like bacon. If eaten raw, the head of the grub must be removed first, as they have a tendency to bite!

In Cambodia, some people eat fried tarantula spiders as a tasty snack. It is a good way of getting rid of them, at least!

Many cheeses can smell a bit, but one of the smelliest is Limburger. It is made in Germany, using the same bacteria that makes the human body smell. This is why it reminds you of stinky feet. Gross!

KEEPING IT SAFE

Honey is the only food that can last forever. In time, food begins to go bad, and germs grow on it. If we eat these germs, they can make us ill. It is important to know how to stop that from happening. In the past, when there were no fridges or freezers, people thought up clever ways to store fresh ingredients so that they would last longer.

For centuries, people preserved and stored their food in ice-houses, cellars, or even underwater in lakes, streams, or wells. Food would have also been preserved by smoking, salting, or drying it.

Canned foods and other shelf-stable products that we all like to eat should be stored carefully. They are best kept in a cool, dry place, away from extreme temperatures.

More than half of the raw chicken we buy contains a bacteria called Campylobacter, which causes food poisoning. Cooking chicken properly stops you from getting sick.

Processed foods, which contain additives such as sweeteners, salts, colorings, artificial flavors, chemicals, and preservatives, are commonly used. However, these are all bad for our health and really should be avoided!

Leftover foods should be kept in the refrigerator within two hours of cooking at a temperature of at least 40°F or below, or in the freezer at 0°F or below. Storing any of these tasty leftovers in the refrigerator soon after cooking will keep them safe to snack on later!

Oxygen plays a large part in the life of any foods you store. If oxygen levels are high, food ages rapidly. Airtight, opaque containers can reduce the oxygen level significantly and will help to keep food fresh so that it can be enjoyed longer and without the risk of nasty tummy aches!

Making sure foods are cooked at high temperatures will kill most germs that could be lurking. Salads and fruit should be kept separately from raw meat, which may harbor bad germs and bacteria.

Dehydrated food is food that has been dried at high temperatures to preserve it. Storing it in tightly sealed containers where oxygen and any other moisture can most effectively be removed increases the shelf life of such foods.

Meats and fish were often cured or smoked in order to keep them edible for longer periods. This was done by hanging the meat or fish over an open fire or soaking in very salty water.

Foods that we want to eat in more than a few days can be kept in a freezer, where no germs can grow on them. Frozen foods usually have to be defrosted before they are cooked. This means letting them warm to room temperature all the way through.

Hard to believe perhaps, but every year almost half the food we produce is wasted. Buying more than necessary can result in the extra food going bad, so we don't even get the chance to eat it!

In the fridge, eggs can absorb smells and other substances from other foods through their shells, so they should be kept separately. Storing eggs safely in their carton or another container helps to ensure bacteria does not spread.

AMAZING BUILDINGS

Whether you live in a busy city or on a remote farm, buildings are part of everyday life. But take a closer look—they're not just bricks and mortar. Some are thousands of years old, some are modern eco homes. Many are breathtaking!

04

MODERN ARCHITECTURE

Modern architecture refers to works of architecture built after the turn of the twentieth century.

One of modern architecture's first architects was Louis Sullivan, who said that "form follows function." He meant that what the building will be used for should help you decide how it is designed.

Early modern architecture is often very simple, with no unnecessary detail. It also uses materials in their natural form—for example, leaving concrete unpainted.

2c

U.S. POSTAGE

Frank Lloyd Wright is often called the greatest architect of all time. Even though he never went to architecture school, he created some of the most important buildings of the modern age, including the Guggenheim Museum in New York.

The Guggenheim Museum in Bilbao, Spain, has been called "the greatest building of our time." It was designed by Frank Gehry, who also designed the Walt Disney Concert Hall in Los Angeles, California.

There are many types of modern architecture. For example, futurist architecture was designed to create a feeling of machine and motion. Expressionist architecture was more artistic and inspired by emotion.

One of the greatest architectural feats of modern times is the Burj Khalifa skyscraper in Dubai. Not only is it the world's tallest building, but it can also withstand wind speeds of over 90 mph on the top floor.

The Crystal Palace, built in 1851 in Hyde Park, London, England, is one of the earliest buildings to use a modernist style. It was one of the first to contain vast amounts of glass supported by metal frames.

The newest architectural movements are new urbanism and new classical architecture. These movements both focus on the impact a building has on its surroundings, including on the environment.

The Pritzker Prize is the most prestigious architecture award in the world. Often known as "the Nobel Prize of architecture," it honors living architects and comes with a $100,000 prize.

CONCRETE & STEEL

Modern concrete is made of water, aggregate (sand or gravel), and cement, which is a mixture of powdered limestone and clay. A chemical reaction between these three ingredients causes concrete to set hard.

The weight of the concrete used on the Burj Khalifa skyscraper in Dubai is equivalent to 100,000 elephants!

The Three Gorges Dam in Hubei Province, China, holds the record for the most concrete used in a single project. It used over 16 million cubic meters. That's six times as much as the Hoover Dam.

The Hoover Dam and the Grand Coulee Dam were the first concrete dams ever built. The Hoover Dam was completed in 1936 and the Coulee Dam in 1942.

M·AGRIPPA·LF·COS·TERTIVM·FECIT

Famous concrete structures include the Hoover Dam, the Panama Canal, and the Roman Pantheon.

The ancient Romans were the first to use concrete as a building material. They mixed lime, water, and volcanic ash from Mount Vesuvius, and called it pozzolana.

During the Dark Ages, which lasted ten centuries, everyone forgot about concrete and went back to building without it.

FE

Steel is an alloy—a mixture of metals. Most types of steel are a mixture of iron and carbon.

C

Reinforced concrete is made by setting steel rods or cables inside concrete structures. This makes them very strong.

Steel was first discovered in the 1700s, but it took over one hundred years to perfect the technique for creating it. It is made by heating iron ore.

The first skyscraper in the world, the Home Insurance Building in Chicago, Illinois, was the first tall building to use structural steel in its frame. Using a steel frame made it possible to build it so high.

The tallest structures in the world are made using steel because it is strong, durable, and easier to use than concrete.

The world record for the most roller coasters in a single park is held by Six Flags Magic Mountain. It has nineteen roller coasters and contains Full Throttle, the roller coaster with the tallest vertical loop in the world at 160 ft.

The most-visited theme park in the world is Magic Kingdom at Walt Disney World, Florida. Over 16 million people visit every year—almost twice the population of New York City.

2876206

The tallest roller coaster record is held by Kingda Ka, located at Six Flags, New Jersey. It reaches the dizzying height of 456 ft. Kingda Ka also has the longest drop of any roller coaster, falling 418 ft.

2876206

The largest water park under one roof in North America is World Waterpark in Alberta, Canada. It covers 225,000 sq. ft. and features the world's largest indoor wave pool, containing 2 million gallons of water. That's one big drink!

The world's oldest operating theme park is Dyrehavsbakken, "The Deer Park's Hill" in Denmark. It opened in 1583 and was built on the site of a freshwater spring said to have healing powers.

The most-visited amusement park in Scandinavia is also the second oldest theme-park in the world. Tivoli Gardens in Denmark opened in 1843 and receives over 4 million visitors each year.

There are around 200 feral cats living in Disney World, Florida. The park lets them stay there because they catch all the mice and rats.

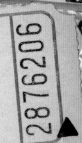

2876206

If you ask for directions at a Disney theme park, the park employee will never point with one finger, as this is considered disrespectful in some cultures. Instead, the park staff points with two fingers or gestures with their whole hand.

The world's tallest waterslide is taller than Niagara Falls! It's called Verrückt, which is German for "Insane," and is located at the Schlitterbahn Waterpark in Kansas City, Kansas. Verrückt is 17 stories tall and has a minimum speed of 65 mph.

The most expensive amusement ride ever built is Jurassic Park, The Ride, located at Universal Studios Hollywood. It took six years to design and cost $170 million. That's twice as expensive as the movie it is based on!

Zumanjaro: Drop of Doom is the tallest drop tower amusement ride in the world. It falls a massive 415 ft. and reaches 90 mph. From the top on a clear day, you can see over 52 miles away!

Disney World is the second largest purchaser of explosives in the United States, second only to the military. Disney World uses them for all its fun fireworks shows.

The world's tallest Ferris wheel is located in Las Vegas, Nevada. It's called the High Roller and stands 550 ft. tall—that's over six stories tall! In its first year of opening, almost one hundred couples got married on the High Roller.

Each year, 341 million people visit US theme parks. That's the same as every single resident in New York City taking 17 trips to a theme park each!

2876206

The Empire State Building was voted America's favorite building by the American Institute of Architects and was named one of the Seven Wonders of the Modern World by the American Society of Civil Engineers.

The world's first skyscraper was the ten-story Home Insurance Building, built in Chicago in 1885. It was only 138 ft. tall, but at the time city officials were suspicious of its safety and stopped construction to investigate.

The White House has been set on fire twice! It was burned down by the British during the War of 1812. Then, in 1929, an accidental fire destroyed the West Wing and Oval Office. Only a few stones of the original building still stand today.

Every year the Empire State Building hosts a race called the Run-Up. Competitors race from the ground floor to the eighty-sixth floor observation deck—that's 1,576 steps. The current record is 9 minutes and 33 seconds.

The White House wasn't given its iconic name until over one hundred years after it was built. President Theodore Roosevelt named it The White House when he lived there from 1901 to 1909. Before that it was called the Executive Mansion or the President's House.

The Pentagon, the headquarters for the Department of Defense, has no elevators because when it was built, the country was trying to save steel for World War II. Instead, to get from floor to floor, everyone uses ramps.

One World Trade Center, also known as Freedom Tower, is the tallest skyscraper in the United States. Including its antenna it reaches 1,776 ft.—in honor of the year the Declaration of Independence was signed.

The oldest known building in the Americas is Sechin Bajo, an ancient stone plaza at the foot of the Andes Mountains near Lima, Peru. It is one of the oldest buildings in the world.

The tallest tower in South America is the Amazon Tall Tower Observatory, or ATTO for short. It's a scientific research tower built in the heart of the Amazon rainforest and stands 1,066 ft. tall.

Las Pozas is a hidden city in the Mexican jungle created by eccentric British millionaire Edward James between 1949 and 1984. It is found over 2,000 ft. above sea level and is full of surreal concrete buildings and sculptures.

Gran Torre Santiago is the tallest skyscraper in Latin America. It is part of the Costanera Center complex, which also includes the largest shopping mall in Latin America.

The Consorcio Building in Santiago, Chile, is covered in trees, so much so that it appears almost entirely green from the outside, turning red in fall when the leaves change.

85

EUROPEAN BUILDINGS

The Tower of Pisa in Italy became "The Leaning Tower of Pisa" shortly after work began in 1173, when the building began to sink on one side! Despite the lean, they continued building the tower for another 199 years.

Florence syndrome is a disorder that causes dizziness, fainting, confusion, and a rapid heartbeat. It is said to be caused by exposure to great works of art and beauty and is named for the city of Florence in Italy.

Palacio Real de Madrid is the official residence of the Spanish Royal Family and the largest royal palace in the world. Despite claiming it as their residence, the royal family only uses the building for state ceremonies.

The most famous fountain in the world is in Rome, Italy. It's called the Trevi fountain, and legend has it that if you throw a coin into its waters, you will be sure to return to Rome.

The Musée du Louvre in Paris is the largest museum in the world. Nearly 35,000 objects from prehistory to the twenty-first century are exhibited there.

St. Peter's Basilica, the largest church in the world, is located in the Vatican City in Rome, Italy, the smallest independent state in the world and home to the Pope, head of the Catholic Church.

The largest scale model of the solar system is the Sweden Solar System. The Sun is represented by the Ericsson Globe, the largest hemispherical building in the world. The rest of the planets are located along the east coast of the country.

The Shard is England's tallest skyscraper at 1,016 ft. high. It is also the tallest building in the European Union, but only the ninety-second tallest building in the world.

La Sagrada Família, a huge Roman Catholic church in Barcelona, Spain, has been under construction since 1882. It won't be complete until 2026!

The tallest building in Europe is the Mercury City Tower in Moscow, Russia. It is 1,112 ft. tall, but it won't hold onto its place at the top for long, as two more Russian buildings expect to surpass it by 2018.

The Atomium building in Brussels, Belgium, is in the shape of an iron crystal magnified 165 billion times. It was built for the Brussels World's Fair in 1958 and is now a museum.

BUCURESTI

The world's largest parliament building is Romania's Palace of the Parliament in Bucharest, which is also the heaviest building in the world. It measures just 282 ft. tall but extends over 300 ft. underground.

The tallest freestanding structure in the Southern Hemisphere is the Sky Tower in Auckland, New Zealand. It is 1,076 ft. tall, and if you're really brave you can jump off the top attached to a wire that allows you to fall 629 ft.

The New Zealand Parliament Buildings are known to locals as the Beehive because of their shape. Let's hope the politicians inside are as busy as bees, too!

The Sydney Harbor Bridge in Australia is held together by 6 million hand-driven rivets.

The Grand Organ in the Sydney Opera House's concert hall is the largest mechanical version of this instrument in the world, with 10,154 pipes. It took ten years to build.

Australia's most recognizable landmark, the Sydney Opera House, was the result of a design competition. In total, 233 people entered the competition, and the winner was at first rejected by three out of the four judges.

The designer of the Sydney Opera House, Jørn Utzon, only won $7,500 for his work.

The design for the Sydney Opera House is based on a ship's sails. It is an example of expressionist modernism architecture, which involves innovative forms and the use of unusual materials.

Angkor Wat is one of the most important archaeological sites in Southeast Asia. It contains the remains of the capital cities of the Khmer Empire, which ruled over most of Southeast Asia from 802 to 1431.

China has three Eiffel Towers! The country is obsessed with imitation and has constructed three towers based on the Parisian icon, as well as a precisely scaled down version of the Sydney Opera House.

One of the most popular types of building in Mongolia isn't really a building at all. Traditional "gers" are large round tents that can house a whole family.

The Wat Samphran Dragon Temple in Bangkok, Thailand, might be the most fearsome building in the world. The tall tower has an enormous statue of a dragon wrapped around it. To this day, nobody knows who built it.

The Chinese have created whole towns based on their favorite places in the world. Thames Town is built to resemble a classic British town, with replicas of actual churches and homes from England.

Beijing's Tianzi Hotel has been voted the ugliest building in the world. The front of the building is made up of three giant, multi-colored figures of mythical gods.

Asian Cairns is a Chinese building project hoping to deal with China's overpopulation in urban areas. It is made up of six tall towers that feature not just homes but orchards and farms—right in the middle of the city.

BRIDGES

Known as the world's most dangerous bridge, the Hussaini Hanging Bridge is a rope-and-plank bridge that crosses Borit Lake in Pakistan. For poor local people it is the only way they can reach northern Pakistan.

Siduhe Bridge in China is the highest bridge in the world—an incredible 1,627 ft. above the ground! That's five times the height of the Statue of Liberty.

When the Brooklyn Bridge was built in 1883, people didn't believe it was safe. To squash their fears, the circus founder P.T. Barnum led a group of circus animals, including a herd of twenty-one elephants, across the bridge to prove it was stable.

The city of Pittsburgh has the most bridges of any city in the world. There are 446 bridges crossing two rivers, the Monongahela and Allegheny, which meet to form the Ohio River.

Tower Bridge in London is the world's most famous bascule bridge—a river crossing made up of two drawbridges that can be raised to let boats pass through on the river below.

The Øresund Bridge links two countries: Denmark and Sweden. The bridge ends with a half-mile tunnel leading into Denmark. During the tunnel's construction in the 1990s, the builders found fifteen unexploded World War II bombs.

The tallest bridge in the world is the Millau Viaduct, which spans a valley in France. It reaches 375 yd. high—taller than the Eiffel Tower—and is considered one of the great engineering achievements of all time.

The Bridge of Eggs was built in Lima, Peru, around 1610. It is held together with mortar that was mixed not with water but with the whites of 10,000 eggs. The bridge is still standing today.

Pons Fabricius is one of the oldest bridges in the world. It was built in 62 BCE to cross the river Tiber in Rome and has been in continuous use ever since. That's one well-built bridge!

The world's longest bridge is 102 miles long. Luckily you don't have to walk across it, as it's a high-speed railway bridge. It's located in East China and is a viaduct, consisting of many arches put together.

The busiest bridge in the world is the George Washington Bridge, which links Manhattan, New York, with Fort Lee, New Jersey. With two levels and fourteen lanes of traffic, over 100 million cars travel over the bridge every year.

A suspension bridge is a type of bridge where the road, or "deck," is hung from cables. The longest suspension bridge is the Akashi-Kaikyō Bridge in Japan, which uses 186,411 miles of cable. That's enough to circle the Earth 7.5 times!

If the US Navy had their way, the Golden Gate Bridge would be painted black with yellow stripes! Other proposals were aluminum and black, but the designer of the bridge decided on International Orange because it was visible through the fog.

The Falkirk Wheel Bridge in Scotland is the only boat elevator in the world. Boats sail onto the bridge and are spun gently around, lifting them to join the canal above.

A bridge that tells you the time! The Sundial Bridge in Redding, California, has a support tower that acts as a giant sundial so you know exactly when you visited.

91

LANDMARKS & MONUMENTS

Most people think Big Ben is the name of the famous clock tower in London, England, but Big Ben is actually the name of the bell inside the tower.

Christ the Redeemer is the largest art deco statue in the world. It stands on top of Corcovado Mountain in Rio de Janeiro, Brazil, and is visible throughout the city. The figure of Christ is 98 ft. tall and 92 ft. wide.

The Vietnam Veterans Memorial in Washington, D.C, is inscribed with nearly 60,000 names. All are men and women who lost their lives during the Vietnam War, the longest war in America's history.

One of Brussels's most famous landmarks is Manneken Pis, a statue of a little boy urinating into a fountain's basin!

India's most famous monument, the Taj Mahal, is made entirely of white marble. It is the world's most famous mausoleum—a place where people are buried in tombs.

Plaster casts of President Lincoln's face were used to make the Lincoln Memorial statue look just like him. If Lincoln's statue stood up, he would be a giant 27 ft. tall!

The Eiffel Tower in Paris, France, receives a fresh coat of paint every seven years. It takes 60 tons of specially mixed "Eiffel Tower Brown" paint to keep the landmark looking good for its 7 million visitors every year.

The people of Kansas City, Missouri, love to read! Their city library has a whole wall designed to look like a giant's bookcase. It's called the Community Bookshelf and features twenty-two humongous books that were chosen by the city's most avid readers.

The Longaberger Company is famous for making handcrafted wooden baskets. They're so proud of their work that they built their headquarters in Dresden, Ohio, to look like a giant basket. At seven stories tall, that's one big picnic!

The Statue of Liberty is hit by around 600 bolts of lightning every year! During a storm, if the wind gets over 50 mph, Lady Liberty can sway up to 3 in.

The Hoover Dam is 726 ft. tall and 660 ft. thick at its base. Enough rock was excavated in its construction to build another Great Wall of China.

The White House is the only private residence of a head of state that opens its doors to the public . . . and tours are free.

The Statue of Liberty was a gift from France to America in 1886, in recognition of the abolition of slavery and the Declaration of Independence. She has a 35-foot waistline and wears a size 879 shoe!

The longest nose on Mount Rushmore belongs to George Washington. His is 21 ft. long, while Jefferson, Roosevelt, and Lincoln's noses all come in at just 20 ft.

Over 90 percent of Mount Rushmore was carved using dynamite. It took fourteen years and 400 men to carve the four presidents' faces, which are 60 ft. tall.

ANCIENT STRUCTURES

Stonehenge is a ring of giant standing stones in England. It was built over 4,000 years ago. The stones weigh twenty-five tons each and come from 160 miles away. To this day nobody knows how they got there!

The city of Machu Picchu in the mountains of Peru is amazing. It's over 500 years old and was built using stones carved so expertly that they didn't even need mortar, which is usually used to glue stones or bricks together.

A huge underground system of tunnels and rooms in Ireland is the country's oldest monument. It's called Newgrange and was built over 5,000 years ago, making it older than Stonehenge and the Great Pyramids.

The Great Sphinx of Giza is a huge stone sculpture of a lion with a human head. It is one of the largest and oldest statues in the world. The Sphinx is missing its nose, and nobody knows how it happened.

The oldest building in the world is Cairn de Barnenez in Brittany, France, a burial chamber built in the early Neolithic era. It is at least 6,000 years old!

Masjid al-Haram in Mecca, Saudi Arabia, was built 1,377 years ago, making it the oldest mosque in the world. Since 2010, it has been expanded to become the largest mosque in the world, too.

The Great Pyramid of Giza in Egypt is the oldest of the Seven Wonders of the Ancient World. Pyramids were built by the ancient Egyptians to bury their leaders, the pharaohs, who were entombed with all their favorite things—even their pets!

The Western Wall is located in the Old City of Jerusalem. It is one of the most sacred sites in Judaism, as it once formed part of an important religious temple.

If you're walking in the Arctic, don't be surprised if you see a giant stone man! These sculptures, called inuksuk, are an ancient form of communication, built by the Inuit people to mark their trails.

Pompeii is a city in Italy that disappeared overnight! It was destroyed in 79 CE when the nearby volcano, Mount Vesuvius, erupted and buried everyone and everything under 19 ft. of ash.

Only two countries in the world feature buildings on their flags: Afghanistan and Cambodia. The flag of Cambodia shows a picture of Angkor Wat, the country's most famous ancient monument.

The Colosseum in Rome, Italy, is one of the city's biggest tourist attractions and one of the bloodiest. It was used in ancient times to host battles between fighters called gladiators, who fought to the death for sport!

The Great Wall of China is the world's longest wall. It is 13,170 miles long! It is over 2,000 years old and was built to keep invaders out.

The Seven Wonders of the Ancient World was one of the earliest tour guides—a list of the most amazing buildings to visit in 200–100 BCE. The Seven Wonders are the Great Pyramid of Giza, the Hanging Gardens of Babylon, the Temple of Artemis, the Statue of Zeus at Olympia, the Mausoleum at Halicarnassus, the Colossus of Rhodes, and the Lighthouse of Alexandria. Only the Pyramid of Giza is still standing today!

ECO BUILDINGS

Animal walkways, or "ecoducts," are an example of how green buildings can help animals. These special bridges covered in grass and trees allow migrating animals like deer, elk, and bears to travel safely over roads and freeways.

London's most environmentally friendly building is the office of the PricewaterhouseCoopers company. Their heat and power system is fueled entirely by recycled vegetable oil.

Two ways we can make our own homes more eco-friendly are to replace our old lightbulbs with energy-efficient bulbs and to put a brick in our toilet tanks to reduce the amount of water we use when we flush.

A zero-energy building is a home or office that creates as much renewable energy as it uses. This means it doesn't increase the amount of greenhouse gases in the atmosphere, which damage the planet.

Yannell Residence in Chicago uses up only 60 percent of the energy it generates using solar and geothermal energy. It's a house that makes more energy than it uses!

A green building is one that doesn't have a negative impact on the environment. Where it is, how it is built, and how it works are all thought about carefully so the building doesn't damage the world.

The Clock Shadow Building in Wisconsin runs on geothermal power. This is when you harness the heat naturally produced by the Earth. You can use geothermal energy to create electricity and to heat homes and offices.

The Bullitt Center in Seattle is the greenest office building in the world. Every part of the building has been designed to protect the environment and provide a healthy working space for its employees.

The India Tower in Mumbai was India's first green skyscraper. It uses the Sun to heat the building and collects and recycles rainwater.

When it's completed, Masdar City in Abu Dhabi will be the first eco-city. The city will run on solar and renewable energy and won't have light switches or water taps, instead relying on motion sensors to turn things on when they are needed.

Sweden is the most eco-friendly country in the world. It uses wind farms in the sea to produce a lot of its electricity, and its citizens recycle.

Crystal Island is a planned building in Moscow. When it is finished, not only will it be the largest building in the world, but it will be powered entirely by wind and solar energy.

An example of a green building is one that uses solar panels to create the energy it uses. This is called sustainability, because it uses resources that don't harm our planet.

Eco-friendly building materials are often recycled or reused. They are materials that don't use up natural resources that can't be easily replaced, or materials that don't take a lot of energy to make.

Green buildings often use renewable energy. This is energy that comes from resources that are replaced quickly by nature. Examples are wind, rain, sunlight, and waves, all of which can be turned into electricity.

BIGGEST, SMALLEST, & MOST EXTREME

Burj Khalifa in Dubai is the tallest skyscraper in the world—twice as tall as the Empire State Building.

The Spring Temple Buddha is the second tallest statue in the world, after the Statue of Unity, in India. It is 502 ft. tall—that's just over one-and-a-half Statue of Liberties high!

As well as tallest skyscraper, Burj Khalifa holds six other world records: tallest freestanding structure, highest number of stories, highest occupied floor, highest outdoor observation deck, elevator with the longest travel distance, and tallest service elevator.

The borough of Manhattan in New York City has the tallest skyline in the United States. Nine of its skyscrapers have held the title of tallest building in the world.

The smallest house in Britain is Quay House in Wales. It's only 10 ft. 2 in. tall and has two floors! The most recent resident of the house was a fisherman who was 6 ft. and 3 in. tall. He couldn't stand up in any of the rooms.

The Petronas Towers in Kuala Lumpur, Malaysia, are the tallest twin towers in the world (1,483 ft.). The sky bridge that links the towers took three days to be lifted all the way up to the forty-second floor.

The world's deepest building is a hotel in Sweden that is 509 ft. under the Earth's surface. It only has one bedroom, and if you need to use the bathroom in the middle of the night, you have to go up 165 ft. to find one!

One of the strangest buildings in the world is Torre Galatea, an art museum in Spain. The roof of the building is covered in giant eggs! The surrealist artist Salvador Dalí, who often painted eggs into his work, is buried under the museum.

The world's largest Gothic cathedral is in New York City. It is the Cathedral of St. John the Divine on Amsterdam Avenue and 112th Street. The cathedral measures 601 ft. long, 146 ft. wide, and has a transept measuring 320 ft. from end to end.

The most expensive home in the world is a skyscraper called Antilia, located in Mumbai, India. It is worth over $1 billion and owned by Mukesh Ambani, the nineteenth-richest man in the world.

HAUNTED BUILDINGS

Salem, Massachusetts, is the location of the infamous witch trials that saw twenty people, mostly women, executed. It is said to be haunted by their ghosts to this day. The city's economy now relies almost entirely on tourism generated by the trials.

The most haunted village in England is Pluckley in Kent. Over twelve different ghosts have been reported to haunt the village, including an angry highwayman who lost his head and the Watercress Woman, who set herself on fire.

The Tower of London is believed to have a royal ghost. Lady Jane Grey, who was Queen of England for just nine days and was held in the tower before her execution, is said to walk the halls at night.

Banff Springs Hotel in Canada is the most haunted hotel in the world. It is reportedly haunted regularly by a family who died in room 873 and by a bride who died when she fell down the stairs.

The Halifax Citadel in Nova Scotia is said to be Canada's most haunted historic site. Staff and visitors have reported several apparitions walking the grounds, including a disappearing soldier who roams the old prison.

The most haunted place in Australia is said to be the Monte Cristo Homestead in New South Wales. It gained its reputation because of the large number of tragic and violent deaths that occurred in the house since its construction in 1885.

Edinburgh Castle claims to be the most haunted castle in the world. Many visitors report being pushed and pulled by unseen forces and seeing ghosts, including a headless drummer boy and a man in a bloodied apron.

Even scarier than Edinburgh Castle are the vaults that run under the city. They are known by locals as the "Screaming Vaults" because visitors get so scared when they walk through them.

IN THIS TEMPLE
IN THE HEARTS OF THE PEOPLE
FOR WHOM HE SAVED THE UNION
THE MEMORY OF ABRAHAM LINCOLN
IS ENSHRINED FOREVER

Perhaps one of the most famous haunted places in the world is The White House. The ghost of Abraham Lincoln was seen by Winston Churchill, the Prime Minister of England, and Queen Wilhelmina of the Netherlands.

If you stay a night in the Château de Brissac in France, don't be surprised if you're woken in the night by the screams of the Green Lady, said to torment sleeping guests.

St. Augustine Lighthouse in Florida has two unusual ghosts—twin girls who are seen running down the stairs hand in hand. The pair are thought to have died on the site during its construction.

MIGHTY MACHINES

From tractors and trucks to rockets and railways, machines make our lives easier in lots of ways. They make it possible for us to travel long distances, they help us with many jobs, and they allow us to explore the world we live in. It is hard to imagine life without them!

05

CARS

The steam-powered tricycle was the first self-propelled mechanical vehicle. It was invented in 1769 by French inventor Nicolas-Joseph Cugnot.

Cars are powered by combustion engines. In a combustion engine, burning fuel inside the engine produces gas that expands and moves the engine to propel the car forward.

Nicolas-Joseph Cugnot also caused the world's first motor vehicle accident! In 1771 his self-propelled steam cart lost control and ran into a wall. The damaged vehicle is preserved in the Conservatoire National des Arts et Métiers in Paris.

The first car released by Rolls-Royce was called the Silver Ghost. In 1907 it set a record by traveling 15,000 miles, proving that it was a very reliable car.

The Model T, made by Henry Ford in 1908, is one of the most famous cars ever made. It became very popular because it was affordable, so lots of people were able to buy cars for the first time.

The power of a car's engine is measured in horsepower. So a car with 120 horsepower is as powerful as 120 horses.

Some cars have up to 30,000 parts—think of all the work it takes to put together just one car!

The term dashboard existed before cars did—it referred to a wooden board that was placed behind the horses on a carriage to stop mud from the horses' feet and the carriage wheels from splashing the passengers.

A modern Formula One car is so fast that it can drive in a tunnel at 120 mph—while upside down!

The first modern automobile was built by German inventor Karl Benz in 1886. That same year his wife Bertha made an important road trip in the car. She covered 66 miles in a single day and worked out lots of bugs along the way.

A man named Ferdinand Porsche designed the Volkswagen Beetle and worked on the Mercedes-Benz. It was his son, Ferry Porsche, who developed the car that carries their name.

Almost 95 percent of retired automobiles in the USA are recycled—that's about 27 million cars every year. Everything from floor mats and instrument panels to steel and aluminum can be used again in new cars and other products.

In 2010 it was estimated that there were over 1 billion vehicles in the world. That's more than double the number in 1986, and the number continues to rise.

Electric cars make so little sound that they can be dangerous. Manufacturers of electric cars add an engine noise so people can hear the cars coming. Nissan and other car companies are working on new sounds that reflect the modern designs of their futuristic cars.

The next big innovation is self-driving cars. They are currently being tested, and Nevada was the first state to allow self-driving cars on its roads.

TRUCKS

Trucks are motor vehicles designed specifically to transport cargo. They vary in size, power, and design. Commercial trucks are very large and powerful and can be used to mount specialized equipment for fire trucks, concrete mixers, and other working vehicles.

The word "truck" was used as early as 1611. It referred to the heavy-duty wheels on the cannon carriages of a ship. In the 1770s it was being used to describe carts designed to carry heavy loads. We still use the word in this way today in the term "hand truck."

There are around 3.5 million truck drivers and 15.5 million trucks operating in the United States.

There are lots of names for the big cargo trucks you see on the highway—big rig, eighteen-wheeler, and semi are all names that refer to different types of trucks—what kinds have you seen?

Large trucks are typically 70–80 ft. long, and their engines are six times larger than a standard car engine.

Driving a heavy truck is very different from driving a car, in part because of the different gear systems. It requires a professional driver's license and lots of practice.

The largest heavy trucks in the world are in Australia. They are called road trains, and they can have up to four semi-trailers hitched to a tractor, making them look like a long train. They can carry up to 200 tons of cargo.

A truck's average turning radius is about 55 ft., and the standard height of a large truck is 13 ft. and 6 in.

The first fire "truck" wasn't actually a truck. It was a hand pump that firefighters pushed on giant wheels. The first self-propelled fire truck was invented in 1841.

A semi-trailer is a kind of trailer that has wheels only in the back. The front rides on the back of the tractor unit. The tractor unit has an engine that powers the whole truck.

Despite their size and the heavy equipment they carry, fire trucks can go fast—up to 60–70 mph. They usually have to go slower when driving on busy streets. When you hear a siren, you should pull over so that the truck can get where it's going as quickly and safely as possible.

In 2011 the Japanese vehicle manufacturer Isuzu set a record with the largest number of trucks manufactured in one year: 447,359.

Most eighteen-wheeler trucks today have ten forward and two reverse gears. They can have nine, ten, thirteen, fifteen, or even eighteen gears.

Semi engines are designed to be able to drive one million miles before needing to be rebuilt.

The engine of a semi is designed to run nonstop. It only has to be turned off to change the oil or make repairs.

AMAZING AIRPLANES

Airplanes are fixed-wing aircraft that are propelled through the thrust from a jet engine or propeller. They vary in shape, size, and wing type, and are used for transportation, recreation, research, and military purposes.

While flying, an aircraft can move through three dimensions. "Yaw" refers to it tilting from side to side, "roll" refers to it spinning around, and "pitch" refers to it tilting from nose to tail.

Have you ever wondered why planes leave long white trails? This is because water heats up and is expelled from the jet engine in the form of gas. When it mixes with the very cold air outside the plane, a trail of tiny ice crystals form.

The Wright brothers, Orville and Wilbur Wright, built and flew the first airplane in 1903. Their plane was based on the designs of Sir George Cayley, who developed the concept of the modern airplane in 1799.

A plane flying at the speed of 400.2 mph will have to fly for twenty years to reach the Sun, 92,955,807 miles away.

The Lockheed SR-71 Blackbird is considered to be the world's fastest manned jet aircraft. It set a record on July 28, 1976, near Beale Air Force Base, California, by flying at 2,193 mph.

Supersonic aircraft can fly faster than the speed of sound. These aircraft were developed in the twentieth century and have been used almost entirely for research and military purposes. The speed of sound is about 768 mph at sea level, which is four times faster than a race car can travel.

An airplane takes off or lands every thirty-seven seconds from Chicago's O'Hare International Airport. That's almost one hundred planes per hour!

Fred Finn is regarded as the world's most frequent flyer—he has visited over 150 countries and flown over 15 million miles.

Black boxes are the electronic devices that record what happens on a plane. Even though they are called "black boxes," they are actually orange in color. If there is a mishap on a flight, they can be used to figure out what happened.

The *Spirit of St. Louis* was the first plane to fly non-stop from New York to Paris. Pilot Charles Lindbergh made the flight on May 20, 1927, and helped design the plane to make the journey. The flight took 33.5 hours.

The Boeing 747, also called a Jumbo Jet, is a well-known wide-body commercial airplane. It is made up of six million parts!

The Boeing 747 weighs around 400 tons, so it needs lots of fuel to get into the air. Its engines pump out 1,000 kilo-newtons of thrust to fly into the air, more than fifty times the amount produced by the fastest car made by Porsche.

Helicopters have spinning rotors, usually featuring two or more blades. When they spin, they create thrust and lift that allows the helicopter to fly. They have one main rotor and one smaller rotor in the tail, which stops the helicopter from spinning in the opposite direction.

Unlike airplanes, helicopters can take off and land vertically, and they can fly forward, backward, and sideways. They can also fly very close to the ground, so they are particularly useful in rescue situations.

Early trains relied on ropes, horses, or gravity to propel them. The use of steam locomotives was developed through the nineteenth century, before diesel and electric locomotives began to replace them in the twentieth century.

Railroads were the main mode of transportation during the nineteenth century in the United States, the United Kingdom, and other developed nations. Trains made it much quicker and easier to ship supplies and goods, and they were used by both Union and Confederate armies during the Civil War.

The world's first steam-powered passenger train began operation on September 27, 1825. It covered about twenty-five miles through the city of Darlington to the northeast of England.

The oldest steam train still running is in India. It is called the *Fairy Queen* and was built in Great Britain in 1855.

Richard Trevithick, an English engineer, built one of the first steam locomotives and showcased it in London in 1803.

Another famous steam train is the *Flying Scotsman*. It traveled from London, England, to Edinburgh, Scotland, and in 1934 was the first train to travel faster than 100 mph.

The B&O Railroad Company started in 1827 as the first railroad company in the United States. Rail workers laid more than 30,000 miles of track for the company, which is approximately 7 percent of the distance between the Earth and the Moon (238,855 miles).

Today, trains are more likely to run on electricity than steam power. They are driven by electricity from overhead lines, a third rail, or a battery. Electric trains cause less pollution than steam trains and take advantage of the high efficiency of electric motors.

The Glacier Express in Switzerland is the slowest express train in the world. It travels over 180 miles of track and crosses 291 bridges, going through 91 tunnels and climbing to the top of the Oberalp Pass at an altitude of 6,670 ft. The trip takes seven hours and passes through some of the most beautiful parts of the Alps.

Most trains have a second locomotive engine that helps keep things moving by pushing the train from the back.

Robert Davidson built the first known electric locomotive in 1837. It was powered by batteries.

There is a railway in India called the Nilgiri Mountain Railway with trains that move so slowly, you can jump off, take pictures of the scenery, and jump back on while the train is still moving—just don't try this on any other train!

There is a high-speed train that travels underwater—the Channel Tunnel carries passengers between England and France and travels underneath the English Channel. It opened in 1994.

A tram is an electric train with a small, enclosed coach that is used for public transportation. Trams were popular in cities around the world by the end of the nineteenth century. Demand for trams started declining as cars became more widely used, but you can still find them in many cities today.

Maglev trains in Shanghai are believed to be the fastest commercial trains in the world. They can reach speeds of over 311 mph. Engineers are hoping to increase the speed to 497 mph by 2020.

Maglev trains move using magnetic levitation. They use magnets to actually float above the ground! Because the trains don't touch the tracks, no friction is created to slow them down, which is what helps them to go so fast.

BOATS AND SHIPS

Boats and ships stay afloat thanks to the principle of buoyancy. Have you noticed that when you get into a bath, the level of the water goes up? That's because your body is pushing aside water to make room for itself. This is called displacement. If you weigh less than the amount of water your body pushed aside, you will float. If you weigh more, you will sink. So even though a cruise ship looks really heavy (and it is!), it is still lighter than the amount of water it displaces.

The first boats used on mainland North America were simple log rafts or canoes. They were used by Native Americans to travel and explore.

The distance covered by ships is measured using units called nautical miles. A nautical mile is based on the circumference of the Earth and is equal to one minute of latitude. It is equal to 6,076 ft. exactly.

All the parts of a ship have their own names. The main body of a boat or ship is called the hull. The rear part of a ship or boat is called the stern. There are also special terms for navigating. Starboard and port are nautical terms for the right (starboard) and left (port) sides of the boat, when facing the front (bow).

The Vikings were very good ship builders. They built ships with flexible sides that wouldn't break when sailing in rough water and used tar from pine trees to make their ships waterproof. This allowed them to travel long distances and conquer many countries.

There are lots of interesting names for types of boats and ships: clipper, junk, dreadnought, man-of-war, longship, galleon, frigate, cutter, and sloop are just a few. What do these names refer to, and what do they make you think of?

The speed of a boat is measured in knots. A knot is equal to one nautical mile per hour, which is equivalent to 1.15 mph. The term knot has been used since the seventeenth century.

The oldest boats that we know about are around 8,000 years old. One of the oldest discovered is the Dufuna canoe, found in Nigeria, Africa. It is between 8,000 and 8,500 years old.

Submarines are highly specialized boats that can operate underwater. They are used by the military, for marine research, exploration, and to investigate shipwrecks.

Americans own around 18 million boats for recreational use in rivers, lakes, and oceans.

Some submarines can remain underwater for months at a time. They overcome buoyancy by filling large tanks with water, allowing the submarine to sink.

The world's oldest international sports trophy is the America's Cup. It began in 1851 and is a prize given to the winner of a series of races between sailing yachts.

The difference between boats and ships is complicated, but in general, a boat is much smaller than a ship. A common saying is, "You can put a boat on a ship, but you cannot put a ship on a boat." Picture a giant cruise ship with many smaller lifeboats on board.

The islands of Hawaii were first inhabited nearly 2,000 years ago by Polynesians who rowed to the islands on large canoes called outriggers. It must have been a very long and tiring journey, but they were excellent navigators and were used to being far out at sea.

A yacht is a recreational boat or ship. The term yacht comes from the Dutch word jacht, which means "hunt."

Royal Caribbean is a cruise ship company that owns the biggest cruise ships in the world—the Allure of the Seas and Oasis of the Seas, which can carry 6,296 passengers each. They are currently building an even bigger one. When it is complete, the Harmony of the Seas will be over 1,187 feet long—164 feet longer than the Eiffel Tower is tall.

ROCKETS

The invention of rockets not only allowed us to travel into space, it also helped us to understand and learn more about our universe.

The world's largest solid rocket is 12 ft. wide and 363 ft. tall—about the length of a football field.

NASA's Deep Space-1 project is based on xenon ion engines. Instead of the hot gases in a regular rocket engine, they thrust electrically charged particles called ions out of the back of the craft.

The world's largest model rocket was one-tenth the size of a real rocket. Launched in Price, Maryland, the Saturn V replica soared to 4,441 ft. before breaking up.

Rockets were invented by the Chinese in the 1200s. They used them for peaceful purposes, such as religious ceremonies, and also in war. The earliest rockets were made by stuffing gunpowder into bamboo containers.

The most powerful rocket is the Saturn V rocket, which was used in the Apollo mission to the Moon. When fully fueled, it weighed 6.2 million pounds. That's the same as about 400 elephants!

The first liquid-fuel rocket was built and launched by Robert Goddard on March 16, 1926. It was fueled by gasoline and liquid oxygen, and the flight lasted for two and a half seconds.

In 1942 the German V2 rocket became the first to travel from Earth's surface to the edge of space. It was designed by Wernher von Braun, who later worked with NASA to build the rockets that went to the Moon. A Russian scientist named Konstantin E. Tsiolkovsky had the idea that rockets could be used to travel into space way back in the late 1800s. He did not build any rockets, but his ideas helped future scientists.

Both jet and rocket engines operate by mixing fuel with oxygen. Jet engines suck in air from the outside. Rockets have an internal oxygen container. This is what allows rockets to fly into space, where there is no oxygen.

Engineers are developing spacecraft that can be powered by the Sun.

Scientists are researching nuclear thermal engines to use in future rockets. The engines would use a nuclear reactor to heat the fuel.

In a rocket engine, two liquid fuels are mixed together and burned to create hot gases that shoot out of the back of the rocket. This pushes it off the ground and into the air.

Most powerful launch rockets use liquid fuel. The Space Shuttle uses hydrogen.

Rockets are machines that produce the force needed to move an object forward. They are used to launch spacecraft, as well as to shoot missiles and fireworks.

The push that lifts a rocket off the ground is called "thrust." The movement of the rocket itself is called the launch. When the rocket is launched, it is said to "blast off."

A typical rocket needs more than one million pounds of thrust for its flight, and it can carry more than 6,000 pounds at speeds topping 22,000 mph. This is equivalent to the power generated by thirteen Hoover Dams, carrying the weight of eight horses.

ROBOTS

Robots seem like modern inventions, but historians have found that the origins of modern robots stretch all the way back to ancient Greece and Rome. Leonardo da Vinci even sketched a humanoid robot in the late 1400s.

Robots usually do repetitive actions or jobs considered too dangerous for humans. For example, going into a building that has a possible bomb, exploring a volcano, or working in factories to build things like cars and computers.

Robots that work in factories are called industrial robots. More than 1 million industrial robots are now in use, nearly half of them in Japan. An industrial robot can have six arms with joints that closely resemble a human arm.

Alan Turing was an English mathematician and computer scientist. He developed a test to see if a machine could think for itself, like a human. To pass the test, a machine must be able to have a conversation with a human without the person being able to tell that they are talking to a machine. This is called the Turing Test.

The first robots used to build cars were introduced in the New Jersey General Motors automobile plant in the 1960s. They were used for moving car parts around.

The word "robot" comes from the Czech word robota, which means forced work or labor. It first appeared in the 1921 play R.U.R. (Rossum's Universal Robots).

Today we define a robot as any manmade machine that can do work normally done by humans. They can operate automatically or by remote control. Robotics is the science and study of robots.

Robotic science is a branch of study that includes three subjects: mechanical engineering, electrical engineering, and computer science.

Professor Kevin Warwick calls himself the world's first cyborg. A cyborg is a cross between a human and a robot. He implanted computer chips in his left arm, which allow him to remotely open doors and operate an artificial hand and an electronic wheelchair.

South Korea is building Robot Land, a theme park dedicated to robotics. It will have a robot aquarium, robot battle stadium, and a cyber zoo. It is scheduled to open in 2016.

In science fiction books, there are robots that look exactly like humans. These are called androids. Although we do have humanoid robots, androids don't exist in real life.

A humanoid robot is one that looks similar to a human. One of the world's first humanoid robots was called Elektro. It was built in 1939 by Westinghouse as a walking machine. It was 7 ft. tall and could say about 700 words.

In the United Arab Emirates, robot jockeys are used in camel races. They started out using non-humanoid robots, but these scared the camels, so now the robots wear hats and sunglasses.

Nanorobots are a new type of robot being developed by scientists. They are tiny robots so small that they can travel through the bloodstream to deliver medicine to a specific part of the body. They are not ready yet, but scientists hope that one day they can be used to treat many different illnesses.

Some robots can act with human-like behavior. This is called artificial intelligence. Face recognition software and computer games that can respond to your actions are both types of artificial intelligence.

TANKS

Tanks are heavy armored vehicles that run on tracks. They were invented during the First World War (1914–1918). The first tanks were very slow—they could only go 4 mph.

In November 1917, all 476 tanks of the British Tank Corps fought at the Battle of Cambrai in France.

The word "tank" is said to come from the secrecy around its development. Everyone except people at the highest levels of government thought they were designing a portable water tank instead of a weapon. The world's largest tank battle was between Germany and Russia at the Battle of Kursk during World War II. Over 6,000 tanks took part!

Tanks were useful because they could drag barbed wire away using grappling hooks, or flatten areas covered with wire so that soldiers could cross safely.

During the First World War, over 6,500 tanks were built by the allied nations (including Britain and France). Germany produced just twenty.

The world's largest tank was called the Maus. It weighed more than 188 tons and had armor almost 10 in. thick. It was built in Germany by Ferdinand Porsche, who also designed the Volkswagen.

The British developed the first tank. It was called the Mark I. It was a rhomboid-shaped vehicle weighing 26 tons, with two 57 millimeter guns and a top speed of 3.7 mph.

In 1942 Hitler approved plans for the world's biggest tank, but it was never built. Called the Monster, it was designed to have a cannon that could fire up to twenty-three miles away.

In early tanks, the commanders could only look around by using a periscope or sticking their heads out the top and using binoculars, which was very dangerous. Modern tanks use thermal imaging to allow people inside to see what's happening outside.

A tank usually has a crew of four to five people. The one with the highest rank is the commander. They tell the others where to go and what targets to shoot. The second in command is the gunner, followed by the loader, driver, and a radioman.

The British designed a tank during the Second World War called Crusader. It weighed 20 tons and had a maximum speed of 26 mph.

The USA wanted their tanks to be easy to repair and maintain. Mechanical reliability was considered very important when they designed their tanks.

Tanks need greater horsepower than cars in order to run. One type of tank, the M1 Abrams, has a 1,500 horsepower engine, more than even the world's fastest car, the Bugatti Veyron (which has a horsepower of 1,001).

To be considered automatic, a machine has to be able to function repeatedly without the assistance of an operator.

Even simple things can be automated. A night light in your house is one example. It comes on automatically when it senses darkness.

One of the earliest and simplest types of automatic control is on/off control. The thermostat in your house is a good example of this. When the temperature drops below a certain level, the heating comes on automatically.

Brazil is the country with the most ATMs. According to the last count by the World Bank, it has a whopping 159,898.

The first automated teller machine (ATM) was invented by Luther George Simjian in 1939. The mechanical dispenser was installed in New York City but was removed six months later because no one was using it. Nearly thirty years later, the first ATM as we now know it was installed in north London, invented by John Shepherd-Barron.

Have you ever wondered how automatic doors work? These doors have sensors mounted above them that emit an electromagnetic or infrared beam and look for changes in the projected field. When the sensors pick up on changes in the beam, the door opens.

Many countries use automation to run their trains, especially city trains used by commuters. The BART system in San Francisco runs a system of around 500 trains that can travel up to 80 mph, with as little as ninety seconds between arrivals. Automation is needed to keep up with such a complicated system.

You have probably seen defibrillator paddles used to shock people's hearts on TV or in the movies. Internal defibrillators also exist. They are implanted in the body and respond automatically to the rhythm of a person's heart.

Automation is very important in the healthcare industry because it can improve patient safety. For example, machines can automatically dispense medication when the patient needs it, even if a doctor or nurse is not around.

Autopilot in airplanes is a good example of an automatic machine. Once it is set up, it controls the path and speed of the plane without the pilot having to do anything. Autopilot doesn't replace the need for pilots, but it lets them to focus on other important aspects of flying, such as monitoring the flight trajectory and weather systems.

Some cars are able to park themselves! They are fitted with sensors and cameras to stop them from bumping into things. This allows them to park perfectly every time.

Self-parking cars are widely available now, but self-driving cars are still in development. Companies like Google are hard at work designing cars that are controlled by voice commands. They are currently testing the cars out on the road to make sure they are safe before they are sold to the public.

Automatic cars are another type of machine you may know. Unlike manual cars, where the driver has to change the gears, automatic cars change gears based on the speed of the car, without any input from the driver.

MACHINES IN DAY-TO-DAY LIFE

We use lots of complex machines in our daily lives, but it all started with what are called the six simple machines: the lever, the pulley, the inclined plane, the wedge, the screw, and the wheel and axle. We still use these types of machines all the time. Can you think of some examples? Look around your house and see how many you can find.

Before household appliances were invented, keeping a house clean was a full-time job. The new appliances saved time, allowing people to work more outside of the home.

Michael Faraday first discovered that electricity can be generated when a magnet is moved in or out of a coil wire. The magnetic force pushes the electrons in the coil to create voltage and current.

John Logie Baird invented the television in 1925, but it took another 45 years before color TV was widely used.

The microwave was invented by Dr. Percy Spencer after an accidental discovery. While doing research on radar technology, he walked through a radar wave and found that the chocolate bar in his pocket had melted!

You have to be careful with microwaves—they can cause explosions! If water is heated in a clean glass or ceramic container, it can reach boiling hot temperatures without bubbling over. Then, as soon as the water is moved, say by taking it out of the microwave, it will boil violently as the heat is released.

The first household refrigerators came on the market in the 1920s. Before that people kept food cold in specially made boxes cooled with blocks of ice. The first electric refrigerator was called the Monitor-Top because it looked like the gun turret on the USS Monitor, an ironclad warship from the 1860s.

James Dyson invented a handheld vacuum cleaner that he claimed had the fastest motor in the world. It reaches speeds of 104,000 revolutions per minute.

Cranes were a very important invention, as they allow us to build skyscrapers. On average, a tower crane stands 262 ft. tall and reaches out the same distance, supported by a narrow steel-frame mast, a concrete foundation, and several counterweights.

The first electric motor capable of turning machine parts was invented by the British scientist William Sturgeon in 1832.

Have you ever wondered how cell phones work? When a call is placed, the phone converts your voice into an electrical signal, which is then transmitted as radio waves and converted back into sound by your friend's phone.

The first personal computer was developed by Hewlett Packard. They released their first mass-marketed PC in 1968.

3D printing has been around for a while, but it is still not used widely. As it becomes more affordable, you will see more 3D printers doing all kinds of amazing things. Scientists are even using them to try to rebuild human tissue!

The world's first mechanical computer, called the Z1, was invented by Konrad Zuse in 1936. His next invention, the Z2, was finished in 1939 and was the first fully functioning electro-mechanical computer.

The first portable computer was released by IBM in September 1975. The system weighed 55 lb., compared with an average weight of around 4 lb. today. That doesn't sound very portable!

123

Some manufacturing plants in Japan have begun to use robots to supervise assembly units. A big Japanese producer of industrial robots, FANUC, has automated some of its assembly lines to the point where they can run unsupervised for several weeks.

Scientists are making serious progress with wireless devices, fitting them with self-contained wireless sensors. These sensors will power themselves with the vibrational or thermal energy in their environment.

Japan has built the world's first laundry-folding robot. Dubbed the "laundroid," it can wash, dry, neatly fold, and sort laundry. The robot can identify what each piece of clothing is and is designed so that it can be built into the closets of the future!

09:00 am
2014-01-01
Search

Electronics company LG has already started to manufacture televisions so thin you can just stick them to a wall. The panel itself is less than one millimeter thick and weighs less than 4.4 lb.

Don Eigler, an IBM scientist, said that in 2050 we will have a laptop with 100,000 times more horsepower than the state-of-the-art machine today.

People are predicting that in the next three years, nearly half of the computers we use will be mobile computers, such as tablets or ultra-mobile PCs.

Researchers are developing television in 9D (9 dimensions), which will deliver entertainment not just through sound and images, but through the senses of touch, smell, and taste.

Futuristic new airplanes might one day have their windows replaced with full-length smart screens, giving passengers the power to surf the Internet, send e-mails, and view the full sky outside.

Scientists are working on ways to use human brain waves to control mobile devices.

According to recently published data, by the year 2050 cars will likely be able to run without fossil fuels, and they may not even require us to take the controls.

Many people spend a lot of time waiting in crowded airports, but aircraft manufacturer Airbus is imagining a future that changes all that. In their concept, people will take their seats in cabin pods before the plane actually arrives. As soon as the plane arrives, the pre-seated cabin pod can be put onboard, saving time and making the process much simpler.

The idea of the invisibility cloak isn't new, but so far the only things we've managed to make invisible (outside the world of Harry Potter) have been microscopic. Until now! Researchers are now able to hide small objects like keys by diverting light around them. What will they hide next?

Researchers in Scotland have invented a slow-melting ice cream. They discovered a natural protein that makes ice cream more stable and less likely to drip down your hand on a hot day!

The world's first vending machine with facial recognition technology was unveiled in England in February 2014. It is programmed to refuse to sell certain products based on the shopper's age, medical records, or dietary needs.

PLANET EARTH

Our planet is an incredible place. With diverse and dramatic landscapes, amazing weather, and spectacular scenery, there are so many of Earth's secrets to still uncover. It is always changing and is rarely calm!

06

LAND AND SEA

The Earth is covered in land, sea, and ice. After the planet formed, the land began to settle into huge shapes called tectonic plates. These plates moved around, split up, and joined together again many times. This created our landscape of land and sea, including mountains, valleys, and rivers. The plates are still moving, but they do this incredibly slowly.

Moving landmasses create caves as well as mountains. The deepest cave is the Krubera Cave in Georgia. Its deepest explored point is 7,208 ft. underground.

One of the United States is moving slowly toward Japan! Hawaii is moving at the speed of 4 in. a year. This is because they are on different tectonic plates.

The Amazon rainforest is the largest tropical rainforest on Earth, and it is thought to have existed 55 million years ago.

Rocks have been found at the bottom of the Grand Canyon that are about 2 billion years old!

More than 90 percent of our planet's plant and animal life is found in the seas and oceans.

How deep is the ocean? The deepest part is 36,070 ft. (6.8 miles) below sea level at the Mariana Trench in the Pacific Ocean, south of Japan. The temperature at the bottom of the trench is between 33 and 39°F.

The Earth has approximately 8.7 million species of animals and 300,000 species of plants.

Seventy percent of the Earth is covered by oceans and seas, and only 30 percent of it is dry land.

Coral reefs take up less than 0.1 percent of the ocean's surface area, but they are home to around one quarter of all the sea life on Earth.

The tallest waterfall in the world is the incredible Angel Falls in Venezuela. It is 3,212 ft. tall.

The Earth is covered in continents and islands surrounded by sea. The largest continent is Asia, and the largest island is Greenland, which is in the Arctic Circle.

Mount Everest, located in the Himalayan Mountains in Nepal, is the tallest mountain on Earth. Its peak reaches 29,029 ft. above sea level.

Life in the ocean changes the deeper down you go! Plants grow up to a depth of about 350 ft. The colors of the fish change too—fish living near the surface are often blue, green, or violet, depending on the depth of the ocean.

EARTH'S OUTER LAYER

Many amazing buildings have been created using stone. The Taj Mahal in India is made of marble, which is a very hard stone.

Granite is an igneous rock, and it is used for making gravestones and statues, as well as many other buildings due to its durability.

The ground is full of metals such as iron, copper, and tin. Metals are strong and very useful for construction. They are also good conductors of heat and electricity. Some are precious and used to make decorative things like necklaces and brooches. These precious jewels are called minerals.

There are 92 naturally occurring elements found on the Earth's crust. Gold is the 58th rarest. The most common element in the universe is hydrogen.

The outside of the Earth is made of different kinds of rock. These rocks contain all sorts of minerals and other materials that we use for building and for making things. All these amazing resources make modern life possible, and humans are constantly looking for new ways to use them.

Gold is a very precious mineral that can be found beneath the earth on all of the seven continents. It is used in all sorts of different places, from banks to false teeth!

The biggest nugget of gold ever discovered is the Holtermann Nugget, found in a mine in Australia in 1872. It weighed 518 lb., which is as much as two sheep!

Pumice is a volcanic rock which is used in many cleaning products such as hand soap and polishes. Pumice is also used in some toothpastes and cosmetic products because of its rough texture.

Pumice is the only rock that can float on water!

Mercury is a very dense liquid. It's so dense that a nickel will float on top of a pool of mercury . . . but don't try this at home!

Mercury is the only metal which is in liquid form at room temperature. Mercury is used in thermometers and barometers to measure tiny changes in the temperature and the atmosphere.

The biggest diamond ever discovered was the Cullinan diamond. It was found in a mine in South Africa in 1905.

The hardest natural substance on Earth is a diamond. This means that the only thing that can cut a diamond is . . . a diamond!

Silicon is the second most abundant element in terms of weight found on Earth, second only to oxygen. Jacob Berzelius discovered silicon in 1824. The discovery led to the use of silicon as a chip in many computers.

MOVING EARTH

You are standing outside, and suddenly the ground beneath your feet starts to move. . . . It shakes more violently, and everything around you is moving, too. It is an earthquake! There are small earthquakes, or tremors, happening somewhere in the world all the time, but when a big one hits, it can be a major disaster.

The Richter scale measures the amount of energy released during an earthquake. A hand grenade releases energy equivalent to 0.2 on the Richter scale. The earthquake responsible for the Indian Ocean tsunami of 2004 measured 9.2 on the Richter scale.

In a major earthquake, the movement of the Earth makes buildings, bridges, and other structures collapse. Everyone is in danger.

An earthquake in Chile caused a city to move up to 10 ft. on February 27, 2010. It measured a massive 8.8 on the Richter scale.

In March 2011, an earthquake struck off the northeastern coast of Japan. It measured 9.0 on the Richter scale. Bridges, roads, and buildings across the country were destroyed.

Japanese mythology says that earthquakes are caused by a giant catfish called "Namazu." In reality, they are caused by the movement of tectonic plates—huge plates of rock that make up the Earth's crust.

It is calculated that every year there are several million earthquakes around the world, though many go undetected.

During an earthquake in San Francisco, California, in 1906, more than 80 percent of the city was destroyed. As a result, people learned how to design cities and buildings to better withstand the shocks of earthquakes.

Some people believe that March is "earthquake month," as there have been two huge earthquakes that shocked the USA during this month. The first one, on March 9, 1957, happened on the Andreanof Islands in Alaska and measured 8.6 on the Richter scale. The second one was on March 28, 1964, at Prince William Sound, Alaska, with a magnitude of 9.2. It killed 131 people and caused $311 million in property damages.

Some of the world's worst earthquakes occur in the Pacific Ocean along a line of weakness in the Earth's crust called the Ring of Fire. This zone encircles the Pacific Ocean, from Alaska down the west coasts of North and South America, and up along the east coasts of Asia. Japan lies on the Ring of Fire.

Tectonic plates move in three main ways. Sometimes, two plates gradually move apart. Sometimes they move toward each other, and one plate gradually slides under the other. Two tectonic plates can also grind past each other in opposite directions. All three kinds of movement cause violent earthquakes.

ERUPTIONS!

Volcanoes are one of Earth's most impressive and deadly displays. Deep under Earth's surface are pockets of hot, melted rock. If there is a crack in the surface, this very hot rock forces its way up and out of the crack.

There are currently about 1,500 active volcanoes identified around the world.

The growth of the volcanoes is due to the accumulation of lava or ash on their surface, which add layers and height.

Magma is a molten and liquid rock that is only found below the Earth's surface. It is turned into lava once it reaches the surface.

Volcanoes are not only found on land, but they also exist on the ocean floor and even under icecaps, such as those found in Iceland.

About nineteen miles beneath your feet is the Earth's mantle. It's a region of super-hot rock that extends down to the Earth's core. This region is so hot that molten rock can squeeze out and form giant bubbles of liquid rock called magma chambers. This magma is lighter than the surrounding rock, so it rises up, finding cracks and weaknesses in the Earth's crust.

Lava flows quite slowly, so it rarely kills people. Most people killed by erupting volcanoes are suffocated by the hot gas and ash that sweep across the land at speeds of up to 125 mph. They may also be hit by flying "bombs" of rock.

It is not just lava that pours out of an erupting volcano. Massive clouds of ash, dust, and poisonous gas are created, too.

In 79 CE in southern Italy, a volcano called Mount Vesuvius erupted, killing everyone in the city of Pompeii in a very short time. Pompeii remained buried beneath the ash and was not rediscovered for another 1,500 years.

Some volcanoes will take thousands of years to form, while others can grow overnight. The volcano Parícutin in Mexico appeared suddenly in a field in 1943, and it grew to over 165 ft. tall within twenty-four hours!

The biggest eruption ever recorded was at Mount Tambora on Sumbawa island in Indonesia in 1815. All vegetation on the island was destroyed, and the sound of the explosions could be heard over 1,600 miles away.

Mauna Loa in Hawaii is the largest active volcano on Earth. From the base to the top it is more than 30,000 ft. tall.

The oldest active volcano is thought to be Mount Etna in Sicily, Italy, which is estimated to be about 350,000 years old. Most of the active volcanoes that scientists are aware of appear to be less than 100,000 years old.

In 1883 the Indonesian island of Krakatoa was destroyed by a series of four massive volcanic eruptions that blew it apart. The collapse of the island created a series of massive tsunamis that struck land as far away as South Africa. More than 36,000 people lost their lives, and the huge cloud of ash it created blotted out the Sun for two whole days.

SCARY TSUNAMIS

A tsunami is a major disaster! Tsunamis are caused when earthquakes happen under the sea. The shock of the earthquake shakes up the water and makes huge waves. They race to the shore, where they can cause terrible damage to people and property.

Tsunami waves are often only 1–3 ft. tall in the deepest part of the ocean. Sailors may not even realize that tsunami waves are passing beneath them.

Tsunamis used to be known as tidal waves, but they are not connected to the ocean tides at all. Tides are partly caused by the gravitational pull of the Moon.

A tsunami is not just one big wave, but a series of waves called a "wave train."

"Tsunami" is a Japanese word that translates into English as "harbor wave."

Only one tree was left standing out of a forest of 70,000 after a tsunami in Japan in 2011. The so-called "miracle pine" was 250 years old.

An estimated 10,000 people died in Hong Kong when a typhoon accompanied by a tsunami took place in 1906.

Tsunami waves surge inland and take everything in their path with them. In Japan in 2011, they reached up to six miles inland. Whole villages and towns were flattened.

Tsunami waves travel across the ocean at speeds of up to 500 mph. That is as fast as a passenger jet.

Caught by a tsunami? Do not panic! It is better not to try to swim against a tsunami, but instead hold on to a moving object and allow the current to carry you.

Tsunami waves can race from one side of the Pacific Ocean to the other in less than a day, so people need to be warned in time to head for higher ground!

Scientists think that a "megatsunami" occurred about 73,000 years ago following the collapse of a volcano off the west coast of Africa. The huge waves caused by the collapse are estimated to have been 800 ft. tall.

The largest tsunami in Hawaii's recorded history occurred in 1946. It killed 165 people.

Scientists in the Netherlands have created a "tsunami generator" that can cause mini tsunamis. They are used to test how dams and barriers stand up against different waves.

Scientists established the Pacific Tsunami Warning System, based in Hawaii, in the USA. Its network of detectors can track quakes that may cause a tsunami.

Tsunamis have a terrible power. They cause total destruction on coasts and islands. The places affected by one tsunami may be very far apart, as the waves spread out across the ocean from their source.

WORLD WEATHER

Today, scientists can predict the weather using satellites in space. These hover 22,300 miles above to take photos and measure temperatures on Earth's surface.

The winter of 1932 in the USA was so cold that Niagara falls appeared to freeze completely solid!

The world's largest snowflake was recorded at Fort Keogh, Montana, USA.
The measurement was 15 in. wide and 8 in. thick—that's larger than a frying pan!

The Atacama desert in Chile is the driest non-polar desert on Earth. Some weather stations there have never received rain.

The coldest places on Earth are at the North and South Poles. In Antarctica, the temperature has been as low as -135.8°F. That is the record for the coldest place ever.

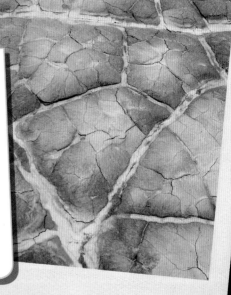

Temperatures are usually measured in the air, but if they are measured on the ground, they can be much hotter.
A ground temperature of 201°F was recorded in Death Valley, California, on July 15, 1972—that's hot enough to fry an egg! The world's hottest air temperature was measured there, too. In July 1913, it reached 134°F!

Millions of lightning storms occur around the world every year. Lightning bolts are incredible discharges of electricity that can reach temperatures close to 54,000°F and speeds of 224,000 mph.

There are two interlinked weather patterns which have a warming and cooling effect on the tropical Pacific Ocean. When the waters become warmer it is called El Niño, and when they become cooler it is called La Niña.

The USA has more tornadoes than any other country in the world, averaging around 1,200 a year.

A lightning strike in the Democratic Republic of Congo killed all eleven members of one soccer team while leaving the opposing team in the match untouched, leading to accusations of witchcraft.

People have often thought that strange weather events were signs of magic or the supernatural. One kind of cloud, called a lenticular cloud, looks just like an alien flying saucer!

Our weather happens in the atmosphere, the band of air around the Earth. Weather can be very different depending on where in the world you live. Most parts of the world have several seasons through the year. In other places, the weather is the same most of the time. Wherever you live, sometimes it is just extreme!

The place where it rains more than anywhere else on Earth is Mawsynram, in India. In a typical year, Mawsynram gets 467.4 inches of rain.

SUPER STORMS

Hurricanes are huge wind storms. They form in warm and wet conditions, usually over the sea in tropical parts of the world. When they hit land, they cause massive damage.

Hurricanes generally occur between June and November when the seas are at their warmest and most humid.

Hurricane Katrina was the largest and third strongest hurricane ever recorded to make landfall in the USA. It caused widespread destruction and damage.

Storm and a hurricane! What are they? If the wind reaches 64–73 mph, it becomes a violent storm. Beyond that it is a hurricane.

The typical thunderstorm is 15 miles in diameter and lasts an average of 30 minutes.

About 45,000 thunderstorms happen around the world every day. Nearly 2,000 are taking place somewhere every minute.

Tall buildings and monuments are frequently hit by lightning. If you are out in a storm, make sure you are not the tallest object around, and never stand under trees.

Ice storms happen when the ground is freezing and the air above it is warmer. The freezing rain covers everything in smooth, glassy ice.

A whiteout is an extreme kind of blizzard, or snowstorm. Whiteouts happen in storms with dry, powdery snow that flies about in strong winds. During a whiteout, it is impossible to see and very dangerous to be outside.

Wind storms such as tornadoes and hurricanes happen when the wind spirals out of control. These are the fastest winds on Earth, and they can cause complete destruction.

Sandstorms are caused when strong winds blow dust and sand into the sky. They travel at around 55 mph and can block out the Sun.

EF1
EF2
EF3
EF4
EF5

The Enhanced Fujita scale is used to find the intensity of a tornado. It's used for the purpose of examining the damage done to man-made structures. The scale ranges from EF0 (Gale), with winds of 65–85 mph, to EF5 (Incredible), with winds over 200 mph.

A tornado is a violently rotating column of air that extends from a thunderstorm and comes into contact with the ground. On April 27, 2011, there were 211 tornadoes that touched down in just twenty-four hours around the United States, with the most occurring in the states of Alabama and Mississippi.

A dramatic thunderstorm is really exciting, as long as you are not out in it. Storms are some of nature's most amazing ways of showing us its power. Darkening skies, strong winds, and torrential rain or snow all remind us that the weather can be incredibly wild.

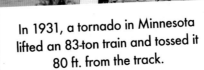

In 1931, a tornado in Minnesota lifted an 83-ton train and tossed it 80 ft. from the track.

POLE TO POLE

At the top and bottom of the world are the polar regions. The area around the North Pole is called the Arctic, while the area around the South Pole is called the Antarctic. It is below freezing and covered in ice most of the time, but there is still a lot happening.

A polar vortex is a massive cyclone which occurs over the north and south poles of the Earth. It extends up into the atmosphere, and it is weaker during the summer and stronger during winter.

The average annual temperature of the Antarctic region is −56°F.

For a few weeks of the year around the summer solstice (June 21 in the Arctic and December 21 in the Antarctic), the Sun does not dip below the horizon, and there is daylight for twenty-four hours a day.

In summer in the Arctic, enough of the ice melts for the land to become visible. It is called the tundra, and it is covered with low-growing plants and flowers.

The South Pole does not have a regular melting cycle. Its ice shelf stays almost the same size and shape throughout the year.

The name "Antarctica" comes from a Greek word that means "opposite of the Arctic."

When you are standing at the North Pole, any direction you can point in is south! In the same way, when you are standing at the South Pole, the only direction you can point in is north!

Some animals in the Arctic can change the color of their fur or feathers depending on the season. Arctic hares are brown during the summer but turn pure white in winter to camouflage them against the snow.

Buried under 2.5 miles of ice in the eastern Antarctic is one of the oldest and cleanest lakes on Earth, Lake Vostok. The lake has been isolated from the rest of the world for at least 500,000 years.

Antarctica is freezing today, but millions of years ago it had a very hot climate. The Antarctic landmass was on the equator.

Many people think that polar bears and penguins share the same habitat. However, this is not the case. Penguins actually only live in the southern hemisphere, which means in the Antarctic region, where they have no natural predators. Polar bears are only found in the Arctic, in the northern hemisphere.

A desert is a place where it hardly ever rains or snows. It does not have to be hot. The Antarctic is the coldest desert in the world.

Polar bears have a great sense of smell and can detect seals (their main source of prey) from over half a mile away.

The largest species of penguin is the emperor penguin, which can grow up to 47 inches tall. The smallest penguin, at just 13 inches, is the little blue penguin!

The Antarctic holds 90 percent of all the ice on Earth.

WHERE ON EARTH?

When rivers flow down the mountainsides and hillsides, it wears down the rocks and soil, a process called erosion. Over a period of time, the water carves out V-shaped grooves. These grooves get deeper and wider, finally forming lowland areas called valleys.

An oasis is a place in the desert where a pool of water is found, surrounded by plants and trees.

Deserts generally receive less than 10 in. of rain a year.

Grasslands cover more than one fifth of the Earth's land surface. They have different names in different parts of the world. In East Africa, they are hot savannahs. In Southern Africa, they are called veld. In North America, they are the prairies, and in central Europe and Asia, they are known as steppes.

The main vegetation found in deserts are cacti and baobab trees. Both are specifically adapted to survive in an environment with little water—cacti store water in their fleshy stems, while huge baobab trees can store up to 26,000 gallons of water in their trunks.

The regions of the world provide many different kinds of habitat. There are forests and jungles, grasslands and deserts. The weather is different in each one, as well as the landscape, but there are stunning geographical features to see wherever you go.

A plateau is a flat-topped highland with steep sides. Since it looks like a table, it is also called a tableland.

The Amazon rainforest has over 2.5 million different species of insect, more than 40,000 varieties of plant, 1,500 bird species, and over 2,000 fish species.

Rainforests grow in tropical places. The weather there is the same all year round (hot and wet). The trees and plants grow thick and close together, and some of them reach incredible heights.

The Sahara is the largest hot desert and third largest desert in the world after the Antarctic and Arctic. The Sahara desert makes up 8 percent of the world's land area, and the entire continental United States could fit inside it!

Mangrove swamps are areas of shrubs and trees that grow along tropical coastlines. The trees have adapted to survive the harsh conditions and salty sea water. Mangroves provide the perfect habitat for many species of mammals, insects, birds, and fish.

More than 2,000 different species of butterfly are found in the rainforests of South America.

The total length of the world's coastline is 217,490 miles, roughly the same distance as from Earth to the Moon, or almost nine times around the Earth!

A bayou is a slow-moving creek or a swampy section of a river or lake. They are home to huge cypress trees, as well as animals such as pelicans, opossums, and alligators.

A CHANGING WORLD

The last two decades of the twentieth century have been the hottest in the last 400 years, according to climate studies.

There are lots of simple ways that we can help our planet. Recycling, walking or cycling instead of driving, and using less water are all good for the Earth!

Are cows bad for the planet? The average cow releases up to 265 lb. of methane, a greenhouse gas, every year. Raising cows also uses up a lot of water and land. There would be fewer cows in the world if there were less demand for beef as food.

Ice is changing all over the world. Eighty percent of the snow on top of Mount Kilimanjaro in Tanzania, Africa, has melted since 1912. Glaciers are shrinking, and ice caps are melting at the North and South Poles. This combination of melting ice and snow has meant that sea levels around the world have risen by 4–8 in. in the last one hundred years.

Today the amount of carbon dioxide in the atmosphere is higher than at any time in the last 650,000 years. This is causing the Earth's temperature to rise.

During their lifetime, more than 50 percent of Americans travel over one million miles in their cars.

In 2010, the number of cars in use on the planet reached one billion. In the United States alone, more than 250 million vehicles are currently registered.

In one year the world emits 33 billion tons of carbon dioxide (CO_2). That many tons could form a giant "CO_2 cube" measuring over seventeen miles on each side. By 2030 our emissions of CO_2 could rise to 40 billion tons.

Most of the man-made increase in the greenhouse effect is caused by the burning of fossil fuels and the resulting emission of greenhouse gases.

Climate change is causing the world's oceans to become more acidic. This may have a harmful effect on marine life.

In the wealthy parts of the world, people have more than enough to eat, but in other parts, millions of people are hungry or starving. Some parts of the world are taking too much, while other parts have too little.

Ancient religions often predicted the end of the world. For example, the Mayan calendar foretold that the world would come to an end in 2012. The truth is, no one knows what will happen, but the better care we take of our planet, the longer it will be able to support us.

Climate change is the increase of Earth's average surface temperature due to greenhouse gases that collect in the atmosphere. This forms a thick blanket, trapping the Sun's heat and causing the planet to warm up.

We release carbon dioxide into the atmosphere from burning coal and gas, from our car engines, and from polluting factories.

We are putting enormous pressure on the world's resources. Everyone needs a safe place to live and to have access to water, food, work, and money. The Earth has limited resources, and the modern world is stretching them to breaking point. Every single person is responsible for looking after the planet.

147

SECRETS OF THE EARTH

Far from being fixed in one place, sand dunes in deserts can move around, sometimes by tens of yards at a time. This can be caused by the wind or dust storms.

The lowest point on land is the Dead Sea, which is found between Jordan, Israel, and Palestine. It is 1,388 ft. below sea level. It is called "dead" because it is incredibly salty, and no fish or plants can live there.

The hottest city on Earth is El Azizia in Libya, where temperature records from weather stations reveal that it has reached about 136°F.

Green-black rocks have been found in the center of the Vredefort crater in South Africa that are believed to be the remnants of a sea of magma. The crater was formed around 2 billion years ago by an asteroid impact and was 190 miles wide. The tremendous heat caused by the impact melted part of the Earth's crust, forming a sea of magma.

Coral reefs have been found thousands of feet below the ocean surface, where they have existed in the dark and freezing cold waters for about 1 million years.

Earth was photographed by the crew of the Apollo 17 spacecraft in 1972 at a distance of about 28,000 miles. The photograph, known as *The Blue Marble*, is one of the most famous images of Earth in history.

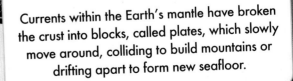

Currents within the Earth's mantle have broken the crust into blocks, called plates, which slowly move around, colliding to build mountains or drifting apart to form new seafloor.

Continents are composed of relatively light blocks that float high on the Earth's mantle, like gigantic, slow-moving icebergs. The seafloor is made of a denser rock called basalt, which presses deeper into the mantle, producing basins that can fill with water.

There is so much ice in the Antarctic that if it all melted away, sea levels around the world would rise by nearly 200 ft.!

The structure of the Earth can be compared to an egg! The Earth's crust is like the shell of an egg, its mantle is like the egg white, and the core is like the yolk.

The Earth's atmosphere forms a sheath around the planet, protecting us from various harmful effects of the Sun. It gives us air and water, and consists of 78 percent nitrogen, 21 percent oxygen, 0.93 percent argon, 0.03 percent carbon dioxide, and 0.04 percent other gases.

The Earth consists of three parts: the crust, mantle, and core. The crust is the outer layer, the mantle is the inner one, and the core is the innermost section. The core is divided into two parts, the inner core and the outer core.

The Earth's inner core is a huge metal ball over 1,500 miles wide. It is mainly made of iron, and the temperature of the ball is between 9,000°F and 11,000°F. That's 6,000 times hotter than our atmosphere!

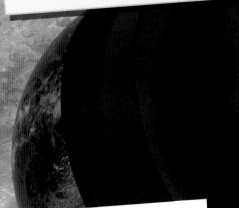

There are many secrets buried inside our planet, and these are revealed by recording and studying seismic waves, studying the earth through our satellites, and studying earthquakes and volcanic eruptions. Scientists are still studying the Earth's structure to find out more about the little blue planet we live on.

The flowing metal of the Earth's outer core helps create a dynamo effect. Dynamos form large magnetic fields which protect the planet from solar radiation emitted by the Sun.

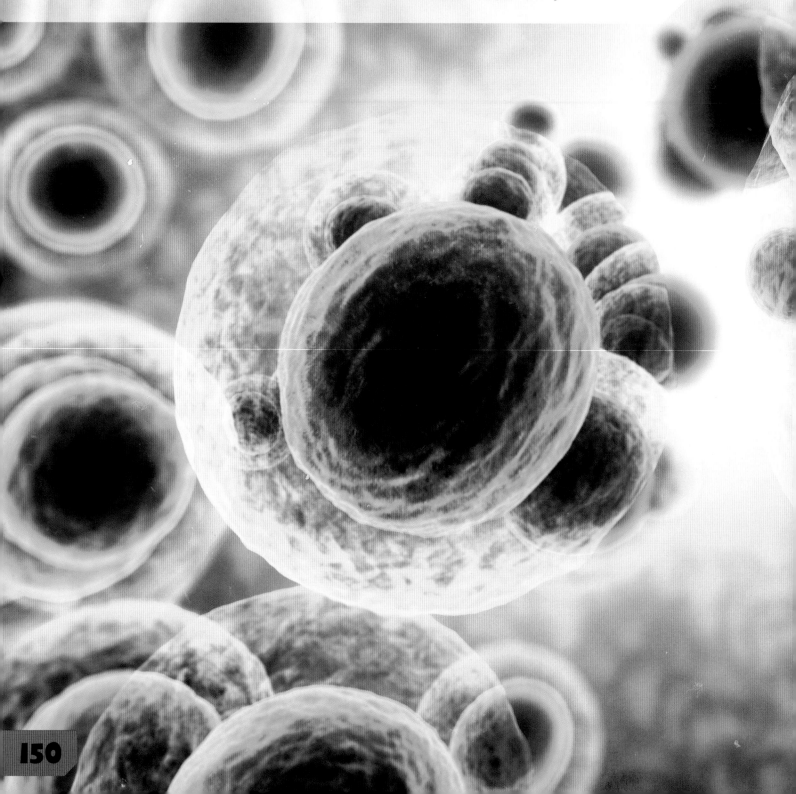

SCIENCE AND TECHNOLOGY

Science helps us to understand the world around us—what it is made of and how it came to exist. We can use these fascinating discoveries to make improvements in technology as well as to help us understand our past.

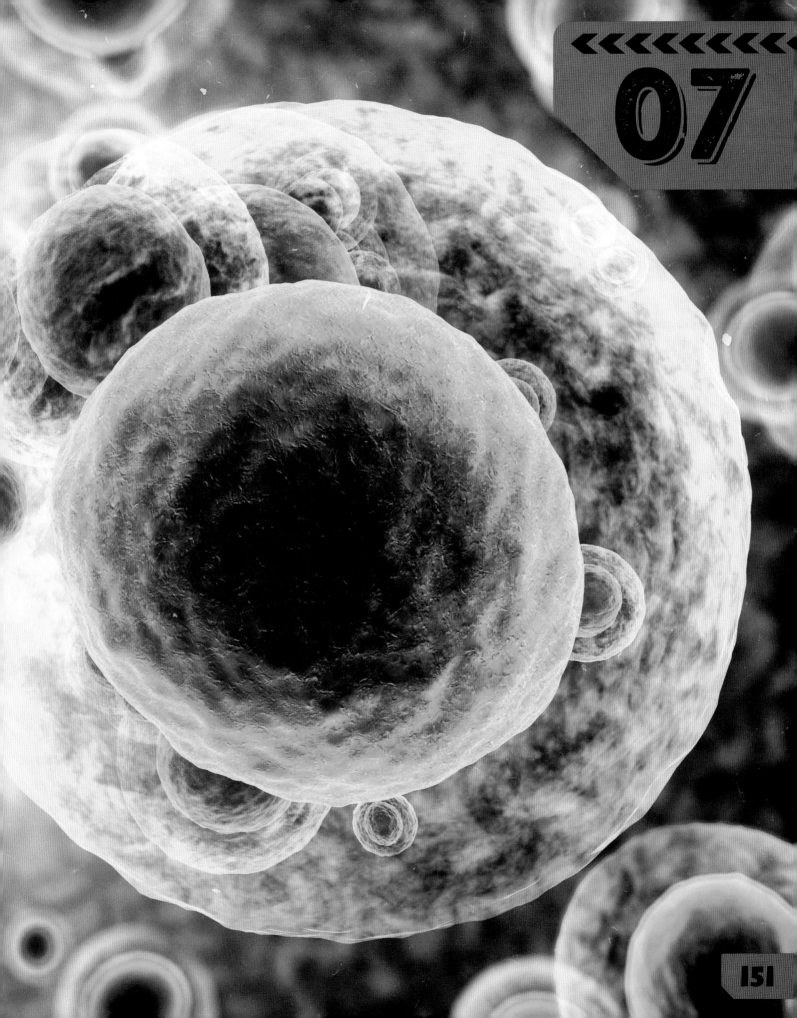

07

WHAT'S THE MATTER?

Everything we can see, touch, smell, or taste is made of matter. Matter is made up of particles so small that we can only see them through a powerful microscope. Most matter comes in one of three states: solid, liquid, or gas.

Changes in temperature and pressure can make matter change from one state to another. The materials that make up the Earth create enough pressure to turn solids into the liquid magma that exists deep inside the Earth.

There is only one substance that can exist naturally in all three states of matter: water. When it is heated, it turns into steam (a gas), and when it is cooled it becomes ice (a solid).

Some kinds of matter can be turned from a liquid to a solid and back again. Water is one example. But not every type of matter can do that. When you cook an egg, for example, it becomes a solid. When it cools down, it does not turn back into a liquid.

Elements are basic substances that can't be broken down into simpler substances. When two or more elements are combined, they create a compound. For example, water is a compound made out of two elements: hydrogen (H) and oxygen (O).

Even though it is so small we can only see it in a powerful microscope, an atom is made up of about 99.999999999999999 percent empty space.

The tiny particles that make matter are called atoms. Hydrogen, oxygen, and carbon make up about 99 percent of the average human body.

When we talk about how different states of matter (solids, liquids, and gases) look and behave, we are talking about their behavior at room temperature. Room temperature refers to air somewhere in the range of 68–77°F. Things change when these substances get very hot or very cold.

Gases flow to fill any container they are put into, but they do not stay still. They have no fixed shape because there is a lot of space between each of their particles.

Do you like the bubbles in a can of soda? Those bubbles are made from carbon dioxide gas (which is a compound of carbon and oxygen) suspended in the liquid.

Liquids form into the shape of whatever container they are poured into, but they don't move as freely as gases do. If you look at a liquid under a microscope, you'll see that they have particles that are close together, but not in any regular pattern. The molecules move around.

Solids are firm and stable. Unlike liquids and gases, the molecules in a solid object form organized patterns. The molecules might vibrate slightly, but they don't move around.

Solid metals have to be made very, very hot before they turn into liquids. They can then be poured into casts to make useful things. They become solid again when they cool down. What sorts of things can be made in this way?

Even in solids there are small spaces between the atoms. The more tightly packed the atoms are, the more dense the object is. Denser objects are heavier, stronger, and harder to break apart. What do you think has a higher density, a brick or a block of styrofoam?

POWER TO THE WORLD

Every second, the amount of energy that reaches Earth from the Sun is equal to the amount a coal-fired power station could make from about 200,000 truckloads of coal!

Enough sunlight falls on the Earth's surface every hour to meet world energy demands for an entire year. The technology is not advanced enough yet for us to use only solar power, but scientists are working on it.

Energy from the Sun is stored in the strangest places. Coal, oil, and gas deep underground are the remains of plants and animals that lived millions of years ago and have been squished down. Those animals and plants contain old energy from the Sun.

Everything you do requires energy. All animals get their energy from food, but plants get theirs from the Sun. Man-made objects, such as ships and cars, need energy too. We get this energy from several different sources.

You and all the other animals on Earth need chemical energy. Your body gets that energy from the food you eat. The energy in food is measured in units called calories.

A calorie is the amount of energy it takes to raise the temperature of one kilogram of water (2.2 pounds) by 1°C (1.8°F).

More than 285 million new computers will be sold this year. The manufacturing of these machines will require 25 million tons of fossil fuels—more than the state of Iowa consumes in a whole year!

Burning fossil fuels releases carbon dioxide into the atmosphere. This is not good for the planet, which is why scientists are researching how to get energy from alternative sources of fuel, like from the Sun and wind.

According to researchers at Google, the energy it takes to conduct a hundred searches on its search engine is equivalent to burning a 60-watt light bulb for twenty-eight minutes.

In a traditional light bulb, only 10 percent of the energy it produces is used to create light. The other 90 percent is wasted heat. This is not very energy efficient.

In the average home, 75 percent of the electricity used by electronic devices is consumed while they are turned off, but still plugged in. This idle power consumes more electricity than all the solar panels in America combined can produce. These devices are called "energy vampires"—scary stuff.

Renewable energy refers to sources that we can make more of or reuse, like wood, the wind, or the heat from the Sun. Almost half of the renewable energy produced in the United States comes from biomass—plants and waste from animals.

Modern wind turbines usually have three spinning blades that can spin as fast as 200 mph.

Before engines were invented, the only way to power ships was with the wind. Ships had huge sails to catch the wind. If the wind did not blow, sailors were stuck until it started again.

We can create electricity from the wind by capturing energy in turbines that spin like big pinwheels. The wind needs to be going faster than 9 mph to generate electricity. Big groups of wind turbines are called wind farms.

AWESOME ELECTRICITY

The movement of electric charge is known as an electric current. The intensity of the current is measured in amperes (amps). An electric current is created from electrons bumping into each other. While each particle barely moves itself, the signal that is created from each small movement moves almost as fast as the speed of light.

The biggest blackout in the United States occurred on August 14, 2003, covering the Midwest and northeastern USA, as well as Ontario, Canada. It affected 50 million people, and in some parts of Ontario, it took two weeks to restore full power.

Electricity travels at the speed of light—more than 186,000 miles per second. If you were going that fast, you would go around Earth 7.5 times in a single second!

Having a very high voltage allows electricity to travel quickly through wires. For safety the voltage is lowered before the electricity travels into your home and other buildings.

Electricity powers so much of what we do. Without it, there would be no computers, lights, televisions, fridges, or washing machines. A lot of the electricity we use comes from burning coal, oil, or gas in huge power stations.

The first reliable electric light bulb was invented by Thomas Edison in the 1870s. It was not nearly as bright as light bulbs are today.

The first street in the world to be lit by electric light bulbs was Mosley Street, Newcastle upon Tyne, England, in 1879.

The microwave oven is the most efficient household appliance in our kitchen. It uses just one-third of the power of most regular ovens.

Benjamin Franklin demonstrated the cause of lightning by flying a kite in a thunder storm, capturing the electric charge from lightning in the kite string. He later invented the lightning rod, which captures electricity to protect tall buildings around it.

When you rub a balloon against your head, you create an electric charge on your hair, which makes it stand up.

Lightning is a discharge of electricity in the atmosphere. Lightning bolts can travel at speeds of 130,000 mph and reach nearly 54,000°F. That is almost six times hotter than the surface of the Sun!

Ever wondered why a bird doesn't get electrocuted sitting on a power line? It's because both feet are on the same power line. If the bird touched another power line at the same time, that would allow an electric current to run through its body.

Fireflies can use the chemical energy from their food to produce light. This light is even more efficient than that of one light bulb. Other creatures can do this too, like the deep sea squid and glow worms.

Even our bodies use electricity—the muscle cells in our hearts contract using electricity. We can measure the electricity with electrocardiogram machines. These machines are used in hospitals to monitor patients.

Coal is the world's biggest source of energy for producing electricity. Coal is burned in furnaces that boil water. The steam from the boiling water spins turbines that are attached to generators, which create electricity that can then travel into homes and businesses.

AN ENDLESS SUPPLY

We do not have an unlimited supply of coal, oil, and gas in the ground. One day, they will run out. We must find new ways to make enough electricity to power our growing world. Research is being done on ways to make more use of different resources, such as water, wind, sunlight, and nuclear power.

Alessandro Volta made the first electric battery by inserting two strips of different metals in a sulfuric acid solution and connecting them with a wire. Batteries use chemical energy to create electric energy and can be used to power things like flashlights, radios, toys, and phones.

Every eighteen to twenty-four months, a nuclear power plant must shut down to recycle some of its spent uranium fuel, and the rest becomes radioactive waste.

Nuclear power uses the energy inside atoms to make electricity. Nuclear power plants create heat in reactors using uranium, a radioactive metal. When the atoms of uranium are split apart, it creates heat that is used to boil water. The steam from the water turns turbines that create electricity. About 14 percent of the world's electricity is made using nuclear power.

Electricity made from the movement of water is called hydroelectric power. The first ever hydroelectric power station was built at Niagara Falls, in the United States, in 1895. It was designed by the scientist Nikola Tesla. Every minute, 379,000 tons of water fall over the cliffs at Niagara—the name comes from the local Iroquois word that means "thunder of water," because of how loud it is there.

There are a few ways to create electricity from the ocean. One way is to use tidal power, caused by the gravitational pull of the Moon. In order to harness tidal energy, a site has to have a big variation between high and low tide. Only about twenty places in the world have the right conditions.

In addition to creating power, wind turbines could one day be able to change the weather. Researchers are working on models to use wind turbines to remove power from hurricanes, lessening their destructive force.

The amount of energy we produce from the wind is increasing. At this rate we will be able to produce one-third of all the energy we need by 2050 using wind power.

Iowa and South Dakota produced about 24 percent of their electricity from wind in 2012.

In 2012 China was number one in the world in wind power creation, but countries around the world are building more wind turbines all the time.

Panels made of special materials like silicon can convert sunlight into electricity. Each house with solar panels stores its own electricity to use when it is needed.

Solar panels are one way to create energy from the Sun, but it's not the only way. Another way is to use energy from the Sun to heat water and make steam, which spins turbines to create electricity.

Geothermal energy plants create electricity by using heat in the ground. Engineers drill deep holes in the ground and fill them with cold water. The heat in the earth heats the water, which returns to the surface as hot water and steam. That steam can then power turbines to create electricity.

Renewable energy sources now provide 22 percent of the world's electricity.

Investing money in renewable energy creates three times more jobs than investing the same amount of money in fossil fuels.

A force is a push or a pull on an object. When you kick a ball, you push it. When a crane lifts a heavy load, it is pulling it up. Forces cause objects to move or to change their speed or direction. Forces can also change an object's shape. Some forces can be seen when one object touches another. Other forces are working all the time, but we cannot see them.

Sir Isaac Newton was the first one to study gravity and force, and in 1687 he wrote three laws to explain them. Physicists still use his three laws for any type of experiment related to gravity and motion.

When an object moves, there is more than one type of force involved. For example, when you kick a soccer ball, the force of your kick moves the ball forward, the force of gravity pulls it down, and the force of air resistance makes it start to go slower.

At the Olympic Games in 2012, North Korea's weightlifter, Kim Un Guk, broke the world record by lifting an incredible 721 pounds. That is like lifting four adult men above your head at the same time!

When you drop something, it falls to the ground. What pulls it down is a force called gravity. Everything on Earth is held down by gravity. You cannot see gravity, but without it, we would all float away!

Ocean tides on Earth are controlled by the gravity of the Moon.

If you drop a hammer and a feather at the same time on the Moon, they both hit the ground at the same time. That's because there's no air resistance on the Moon, while on Earth air resistance greatly slows down the feather.

The standard gravity from Earth is 1 g-force. When riding a roller coaster you may feel a g-force of 4 or 5. That's the feeling you get when you are pushed back into your seat. Fighter pilots or astronauts may feel even more.

Another force that is important to us is magnetic force. It attracts some metals, especially iron and steel. A magnet has two ends, or poles, called north and south. A north pole of one magnet will attract the south pole of another magnet, but if you put two north or two south poles together, the magnets will push away from each other.

Like the Moon, Mars has less gravity than Earth because it is smaller and has less mass. If you weigh 100 lb. on Earth, you would only weigh 38 lb. on Mars.

A hurricane is a circular tropical storm that displays a lot of force, creating heavy wind, rain, flooding, and even tornadoes. Hurricanes in the northern hemisphere move counterclockwise around the "eye," or center, of the storm. In the southern hemisphere, the winds turn in the opposite direction.

Depending on where they are in the world, hurricanes can also be called cyclones or typhoons. No matter where it starts, to be a hurricane a storm must have winds blowing at least 74 mph—that's faster than a car on the highway!

Friction is a type of force that resists motion. It is created when one object rubs against another. When you use the brakes on your bike, friction is what slows you down. The brake rubs against the bike wheel, causing it to spin more slowly.

Springs and elastic are also types of force. If you stretch them out, they spring back with the same force you created by pulling on them.

Drag is a force that decreases the velocity (speed) of an object. Thrust is a force that increases the velocity of an object.

LIGHT FOR ALL

Some solids can let light pass through them. They are called transparent. Clear glass is transparent, but frosted glass only lets some light through. We call it translucent.

Light travels in waves. It moves incredibly fast, at a speed of 186,000 miles per second—faster than anything else in the universe. Light from the Sun takes approximately eight minutes to travel the 93 million miles to Earth.

Light is a form of energy. It can travel freely through the air. When you wake up in the morning, you can see the world around you because it is lit up by the Sun, even if it is a cloudy day. At night, when the Sun has set, we have to make our own light, using electricity or flames.

Light travels in straight lines, so it cannot go around objects. When an object blocks light, a dark area forms behind it. This is how shadows are made.

Light travels through different kinds of matter such as glass, water, and air at different speeds. The refractive index of an object tells us how much light bends passing through it, and it can also tell us how much slower light travels through an object.

Auroras are amazing, colorful light formations that appear in the night skies at high latitudes in the northern and southern hemispheres. They are caused by electrically charged particles from solar winds colliding with gases in our atmosphere. In the northern hemisphere they are called aurora borealis, and in the southern hemisphere they are called aurora australis.

Light takes 1.255 seconds to get from Earth to the Moon.

Astronomy is the study of everything outside of the Earth's atmosphere, like the planets and the stars. People who study astronomy are called astronomers. They use light-years to measure the distances between objects in space that are very far apart.

The closest star to the Sun is Proxima Centauri. It is 4.2 light-years from Earth—that's more than 25 million miles!

A light-year is the distance that an object moving at the speed of light travels in one year. More accurately, it is the distance light travels in a vacuum. A vacuum is a space without any matter in it. This is important because matter, such as air, would create friction, which would affect the speed.

Anything that gives off light, such as a flashlight, is luminous. Most things are not luminous. They seem bright because they are lit up by something else. The Sun is luminous, but the Moon is not. It only seems to shine because its surface reflects light from the Sun.

There is a light bulb in California that has reportedly been burning since 1901. It is the world's longest-lasting light bulb.

Plants need light so they can grow. They use energy from sunlight to convert carbon dioxide into food. This process is called photosynthesis.

Some people start to sneeze when they are exposed to bright light. This is called the photic sneeze reflex, and it affects 18 to 35 percent of the population.

Sunlight can reach a depth of about 262 ft. in the ocean. That's almost the height of the Statue of Liberty (305 ft.). Far below that depth, bioluminescent fish glow to attract prey in the pitch black water.

RAINBOW WORLD

Colors are an important part of astronomy because they can be used to measure how big a star is. Bigger stars look blue and smaller stars look yellow.

All around us are thousands of different colors and shades, and our eyes are very good at telling them all apart. How many different colors can you find on this page?

The three primary colors of red, blue, and yellow can be combined in different ways to make every color. Mixing red and blue makes purple, and red and yellow make orange. What combinations have you made?

The color orange makes you hungry. Restaurants use this to make you want to stop and eat their food. Next time you are out, notice how many roadside restaurants have orange, red, and yellow signs.

Humans can only see shades from red to violet. Some insects can see even more colors past violet. These are called ultraviolet.

The parts of our eye that allow us to see colors are called cones. We have red, blue, and green cones. Dogs and cats only have blue and green cones, so they can't see as many colors as we can.

You can use a prism to separate light into different wavelengths. Each wavelength is a different color: red, orange, yellow, green, blue, indigo, and violet.

Color-blindness is a condition that makes it difficult to tell colors apart. Some people can't see any colors at all. Color-blindness is an inherited trait, meaning it can be passed down from parent to child.

When the Sun sets, the light has to travel through more of Earth's atmosphere before you can see it. The molecules that the light passes through scatter the blue and violet light, which is why we see sunsets as pink, orange, and red.

The color red is often used to warn people or draw their attention to something. It is used in traffic signals, on stop signs, and on fire extinguishers. Where else have you seen red used in this way?

If you watch a sunrise or sunset, you might also see a green flash. This is when the Sun suddenly turns green. It sometimes happens just after sunrise, and just before sunset. You can only see it on a really clear day, and you'll have to be lucky—blink and you'll miss it! But be careful, it is dangerous to look directly at the Sun.

Violet has the shortest wavelength. Red has the longest.

If you look at a rainbow from up in a plane, it appears as a complete circle around the Sun.

Studies have shown that more people choose blue as their favorite color than any other. But did you know that many ancient people, including the Greeks, had no word for blue? It was only after the Egyptians invented blue dye that people began to consider blue to be a color at all.

The color black is created by the absence of color. White is created when all the colors are combined into one.

TAKING PICTURES

When cameras were first invented, it took a lot longer to take a picture than it does now. The oldest picture in the world is called *View from the Window at Le Gras*. It was taken in 1826 by photographer Nicéphore Niépce at his estate in France. It took eight hours to take the picture!

The first cameras were invented by Frenchman Louis Daguerre and Englishman William Henry Fox Talbot at around the same time, in 1837. But they were very large and heavy, and not practical for the public to use.

It used to take so long to take a photograph that children couldn't sit still. To help keep them calm, mothers would sometimes be in the photograph, hiding behind objects or draped in fabric to look like a chair!

Even though cameras weren't developed until the 1800s, the idea for them has existed since ancient times. The ancient Greeks and Chinese used a device called the camera obscura to project an image onto a screen.

Photos are made blurry by tiny camera movements that happen while the shutter is open. This happens more often when trying to take photos in darker places, because the shutter has to stay open longer to collect enough light for the photo. You can avoid this by using a tripod—unlike you, it can hold perfectly still!

The first aerial photograph was taken by French photographer Gaspard-Félix Tournachon in 1858. He took the photo from a hot air balloon 260 ft. above the ground. This was a very difficult job. It took three years of experiments to get the first photograph, and he had to bring an entire dark room up in the balloon with him!

George Eastman designed a camera that was much smaller and easier to use than the early models. He started selling his Kodak camera in 1888. It was a very simple box camera with a fixed-focus lens and single shutter speed.

Today's cameras are mostly digital. They do not record photos onto plastic film. Instead, they store the images on a light-sensitive sensor inside the camera. The first digital cameras were introduced to the public in 1988.

When you press the button on your camera to take a photo, it briefly opens the shutter (like opening a curtain), allowing light to pass through the lens on to the film or sensor inside.

There are twelve Hasselblad cameras on the surface of the Moon. They were left behind on the first Moon landing to make room so the astronauts could bring back lunar rocks.

Cameras are used to take pictures. They can be still pictures, like photos, or moving pictures, like film. Cameras are complicated inside, but basically, they catch the light given off by whatever they are pointed at. They use lenses to focus this light to make an image that can be saved and looked at again.

Today taking photos is so easy that we can do it all the time. In fact, today we take as many photos every two minutes as the entire world did in the whole of the 1800s.

People upload 350 million photos to Facebook every day, and around 40 million photos to Instagram. That's a lot of pictures!

A film camera records a lot of images, one after the other, on very long strips of plastic film. They take twenty-five separate pictures every second. When the series of images is shown quickly, they all seem to "join up," and the scene appears to move.

Traditional film cameras record images on a long strip of plastic. The plastic strip is coated with chemicals called silver halide crystals that are sensitive to light.

HEAR THAT?

Our world is almost never silent. By day we hear the voices of everyone around us, the sounds of cars and planes, machines, and music. Even at night there are animal and bird sounds and the sound of the wind in the trees. Sound is another kind of energy.

Sound is present in an invisible form that we cannot see. Like light, it travels in waves. Those waves vibrate small bones in your ear called the hammer, anvil, and stirrup. They are the smallest bones in your body—all together, they are only the size of a pea!

The units used for measuring sound are called decibels (dB). Conversation is about 50 dB. A loud rock concert is about 110 dB. Anything louder than 140 dB can damage your hearing.

Some hard materials reflect sound, bouncing it back in the direction it came from. This is called an echo.

Sounds are tiny vibrations. Sound requires the presence of three things: something to make the sound, a material for the sound vibrations to move through, and something to receive the sound.

A whip makes a snapping sound when you crack it because its tip is moving faster than the speed of sound. The sound is a mini sonic boom.

Sound cannot travel as fast as light, but it is still incredibly fast. It travels faster through warm air than cold air. At 32 °F, sound travels at 740 mph. It can travel a mile in just five seconds!

There is a tribe in Africa, the Maabans, that lives a very quiet lifestyle and is very sensitive to sound. Even old people in the tribe can hear a whisper from distances as long as a baseball field.

Pitch refers to how frequently the particles in air vibrate when a sound is made. The faster the particles vibrate, the higher the pitch. A tea kettle makes a very high-pitched noise. A big drum makes a low-pitched noise.

Some planes can fly even faster than the speed of sound. When they do, they create a shock wave that creates a noise like thunder. This is called a sonic boom, and sometimes it can be heard by people on the ground. A sonic boom from a plane can be powerful enough to break windows.

When a plane makes a sonic boom, the sound waves disturb the water particles in the air, and a strange cloud forms around the plane.

In space there is no air, so there is nothing for sound waves to travel through. This means there is no sound, so space is totally silent.

Pitch is measured in hertz, which is a count of the number of vibration cycles per second. Experiments have proven that a healthy young person can hear sounds traveling in a frequency range between 20 and 20,000 hertz.

Older people cannot hear some high-pitched sounds. This is due to the natural aging of the cells in our ears, called presbycusis.

Did you know that elephants can detect sound vibrations from 2 miles away? They detect the vibrations with their sensitive trunks and feet.

Bats use a special sense called echolocation. They listen to echoes of their ultrasonic calls to find food and avoid obstacles while flying at night. They "see" with their ears!

Blue whales are the loudest animals. They produce sounds that can reach 188 decibels—loud enough to be heard from 530 miles away.

SOUND OF MUSIC

Music is a kind of arranged sound. People have learned how to make particular sounds, and we put them together in a way that pleases us. Maybe you love pop music or classical music, or music from countries around the world. Wherever it comes from, it can make you want to dance!

A Stanford study showed that music engages areas of the brain that control our ability to pay attention, make predictions, and update events in our memory.

Making sounds louder is called amplification. Many musical instruments have a part that amplifies their sound. On a guitar, for example, the instrument's large wooden body amplifies the sound made by the strings.

Learning music is great for your brain. Children who study music tend to have larger vocabularies and more advanced reading skills than those who don't.

The highness or lowness of a sound is called its pitch. Musical notes are sounds with a particular pitch. In a stringed instrument, longer strings make sounds with a lower pitch than shorter strings. That is why a double bass makes lower notes than a violin.

When a violin is played, the hairs on the bow are pulled or pushed across the strings on the violin. This makes the strings vibrate, creating sound.

Listening to relaxing music can make cows produce more milk. A 2001 study involving 1,000 cows exposed them to fast, slow, or no music for twelve hours a day over a nine-week period to find these results.

The Challen Concert Grand is the world's largest piano. It is about 11 ft. long and weighs more than a ton.

Songs that get stuck in your head are called "earworms." But don't worry, it's just an expression!

A symphony is a form of music characterized by a harmonious combination of elements, in which a large orchestra plays a long musical composition.

Playing music can make plants grow bigger. Dr. T. C. Singh showed that after playing Indian music near balsam plants, these plants grew 20 percent taller in height and had 72 percent more biomass.

We all know that music can affect our emotions, but did you know it can change your body as well? Fast music makes your heartbeat and breathing accelerate, while slow music has the opposite effect.

A drum has a tight skin that vibrates when it is hit. The air inside the drum vibrates, making the sound.

The bass drum makes up one-third of the total power of a seventy-five piece orchestra.

Music can help people with serious illness such as Parkinson's and Alzheimer's. Music can also help with bradykinesia, which is a difficulty initiating movement. The music triggers neurons that translate the music into organized movement. Music therapy can also help restore the loss of language in patients with impaired speech caused by brain injury after sustaining a stroke.

171

OUR UNIVERSE

Our planet may seem huge, but it is just a tiny speck floating in the vastness of space. Discovering what else is out there is an exciting challenge, and it started hundreds of years ago with people staring up at the stars.

08

SPACE AND BEYOND

Black holes are areas of space where matter has collapsed in on itself. The result is a huge amount of mass in an incredibly small area. The pull of gravity in this area is so strong that nothing can escape from it, not even light.

The universe is everything that exists, from Earth to the most distant parts of space. It is almost impossible to imagine how big and how awesome it is. The universe is mostly filled with empty space, but it also contains billions of galaxies, stars, and other wonders.

The universe is full of an unknown substance called "dark matter." Dark matter makes up about 25 percent of all the matter in the universe.

The universe has been expanding since it first came into existence, and it is still expanding today. Everything is moving away from everything else. We know the universe is at least 93 billion light years across, but this distance is increasing all the time.

In 1964, scientists predicted that a particle exists that would help explain how the universe works. In 2012, they found the Higgs boson particle by smashing together tiny protons in a machine called the Large Hadron Collider, which cost $10 billion to build!

Scientists think the universe began with an event called the Big Bang. This was a huge explosion that created all the matter and energy in the universe. The Big Bang took just a fraction of a second, but it was the beginning of time and space.

Have you ever wondered how old the universe is? No one knows its exact age, but scientists think it is at least 13.8 billion years old—in fact, the universe is the oldest thing in existence!

Outer space begins about 62 miles above Earth, where the shell of air around our planet disappears. There is no air to scatter sunlight, so space looks like a black blanket dotted with millions of stars.

Neutron stars are the smallest and densest objects in our universe. They are formed when stars collapse after a supernova. They can weigh twice as much as our Sun but are only about 14 miles wide.

You could fit 1 million Earths inside our Sun, but it is still technically classed as a dwarf star!

Is there extraterrestrial life out there in the universe? There is evidence that Mars could once have been warmer and wetter and could have supported life.

Sagittarius B2 is a cloud of dust and gas that is found in the center of the Milky Way . . . and also a great location for a galactic bar! It contains 1 billion billion billion liters of "vinyl alcohol," which is a very important organic compound that is critical to the existence of life.

Do you know which star is the biggest in the universe? "NML Cygni" is a hypergiant found in the constellation of Cygnus the swan and is one of the largest stars currently known.

Mount Everest is not the king of the solar system. Olympus Mons is a massive volcano on Mars and is the biggest mountain in our solar system. It is 374 miles in diameter (approximately the same size as the state of Arizona) and 16 miles tall.

Have you ever wished that there were more hours in the day? The Earth's rotation slows down by about 1.4 milliseconds every century. A day lasted for 23 hours when dinosaurs ruled our earth.

STARS IN YOUR EYES

Stars live for a very long time. They take billions of years to die. Once a star has burned all its fuel, it grows bigger and bigger and becomes a "red giant."

A supergiant is the largest known type of star, and some are almost as large as our entire solar system! These stars are rare. When supergiants die, they often explode into supernovae, producing black holes.

Eta Carinae is one of the largest stars in our galaxy and is known as a "hypergiant." It is 10 million times brighter than our Sun. Pistol, another hypergiant, is even brighter than Eta Carinae.

Our galaxy, the Milky Way, was formed when smaller galaxies came together to make a bigger one.

One of the smallest stars in our galaxy is VB10. It is only 20 percent larger than Jupiter.

The twinkling of stars in the sky is caused by Earth's atmosphere. The atmosphere bends and breaks up the faint light from the stars before it reaches our eyes.

A nebula is a huge cloud of gas and dust in space. The gas in nebulae (the plural of nebula) is mostly hydrogen gas.

Some red giants grow into supergiants. After a few million years, they blow up in an explosion called a supernova. One of the last supernovae in our galaxy took place about 400 years ago. It was 13,000 light years from Earth.

There are about 400 billion stars in our galaxy. It is almost impossible to count how many stars there are in the universe because there are so many!

White dwarfs are the final evolutionary state of all stars (including our Sun). They are very hot when they form, but over billions of years they cool down and lose energy.

The Milky Way moves through space at a velocity of about 343 miles per second.

The Hubble Space Telescope lives in space and orbits the Earth. It has found lots of galaxies since it first started looking into deep space in 1990.

A blue giant is a huge, very hot, blue star. They can grow to five to ten times the size of our Sun.

OUR SOLAR SYSTEM

Our solar system lies in one of the arms of a large spiral galaxy called the Milky Way. It is about halfway out from the middle of the galaxy. It consists of a star (the Sun) and eight planets that orbit the Sun. The planets are Mercury, Venus, Earth, Mars, Jupiter, Saturn, Uranus, and Neptune.

The Earth takes a day to rotate on its axis; however, the Milky Way rotates once every 200 million years.

The Milky Way contains over 400 billion stars. Light, which travels incredibly fast, can take nearly 100,000 years to cross from one side of the galaxy to the other.

When our galaxy was created, scientists believe that the Sun was formed first, followed by a flat disc of dust, which eventually formed all the planets we know today, including Earth.

The solar system was formed approximately 4.6 billion years ago, and it is thought to have evolved from the collapse of a huge dust cloud.

Jupiter is the largest planet in our solar system and is known mainly for its "Great Red Spot," which is actually a huge storm, three times the size of Earth, on Jupiter's surface.

Pluto is smaller than the USA. According to the best current estimates, Pluto is just over 1,400 miles across, slightly over half the width of the USA.

The largest moon in the solar system is Ganymede, which orbits around Jupiter. It is about twice the size of our Moon and is made of rocks and ice.

Until recently, the farthest known planet was Pluto, an icy world at the edge of the solar system. Scientists now think it is too small to be called a true planet. It is even smaller than our Moon. Pluto is now called a dwarf planet, and more of them have been found.

One of the most heavily cratered objects in the solar system is Mimas, a moon of Saturn.

The Kuiper Belt is a region of the solar system beyond the planets, stretching away from the orbit of Neptune out into space. It contains comets and asteroids and is similar to an asteroid belt, but is 20 times wider and 20–200 times as massive.

The Oort Cloud lies far away from Kuiper Belt and theoretically extends from 5,000 to 100,000 times the distance of Earth to the Sun. It is home to up to 2 trillion icy objects, according to NASA.

Mercury, Venus, Earth, and Mars are called "terrestrial planets" because they have solid, rocky surfaces and are closer to the center of the solar system. Jupiter, Saturn, Uranus, and Neptune are the four outer planets, also known as the "gas giants." These are mostly made up of gases and are more massive than the inner planets.

Some scientists consider Jupiter to be an important planet for the Earth's safety. The reason is that its huge size and gravitational pull act as a protective barrier that shields the Earth from space debris, pulling away any dangerous objects before they reach our planet.

A comet is an icy body that releases gas or dust. Astronomers have found that comets are the residues from the gas, dust, ice, and rocks that initially formed the solar system.

OUR SUN

The Sun radiates heat and a steady stream of charged particles known as the solar wind, which blows about 280 miles per second throughout the solar system.

If the Moon gets directly between Earth and the Sun, it blocks the Sun's light on Earth for a few moments, and it goes dark in the daytime. This is called an eclipse.

The Sun rotates on its axis once every 25.38 Earth days, or 609.12 hours.

In 1976, *Helios 2* came within 37 million miles of the Sun. This is the closest approach to the Sun by any spacecraft.

The Sun provides a vital ingredient for most of the life on Earth. Without the energy provided through sunlight, vegetation cannot grow, and without vegetation animals do not have a source of nourishment.

The Sun is a star, but we never see it at night! It is a huge ball of super-hot gas. It produces the light and heat that make life on our planet possible. Without it, our world would be frozen and dark.

The Sun is so big that it accounts for over 99 percent of the mass (weight) in the solar system. That means that all the planets put together, as well as all the moons and asteroids, make up less than 1 percent of the solar system's mass.

It is estimated that the Sun will continue to burn for about 130 million years, when it will stop burning hydrogen and instead start burning helium. During this process, it will expand to such a size that it will engulf Mercury, Venus, and Earth and become a red giant star.

The Sun generates huge amounts of energy by combining hydrogen nuclei into helium. This process is called nuclear fusion.

Five million tons of hydrogen are consumed by the Sun every second. This helps to create the Sun's composition of 75 percent hydrogen, 23 percent helium, and 2 percent heavier elements.

The Sun is the closest star to Earth. It is about 93 million miles away from our planet—that's 3,750 times the circumference of the Earth!

The Sun has been worshiped in many ancient cultures. The ancient Egyptians worshiped it as the god Ra, and the Aztecs called it Tonatiuh.

The Sun is so far away that its light takes about eight minutes to reach Earth. When we see a sunset, it actually happened about eight minutes ago.

The temperature of the Sun's core is around 27 million degrees Fahrenheit!

In the sixteenth century, Nicolaus Copernicus argued that it was the Earth that orbited around the Sun rather than the other way around. However, Copernicus's view of the solar system wasn't accepted for many years until Isaac Newton formulated his laws of motion.

EARTH AND MOON

Magma is the hot liquid rock under the surface of the Earth. It is known as lava after it comes out of a volcano.

The closest object to Earth is its moon. The Moon is much nearer to Earth than any of the planets. It travels around Earth and makes one complete orbit of our planet every 27.3 days.

The Moon is in synchronous rotation with the Earth, meaning the same side is always facing the Earth.

Earth is the only planet with an atmosphere that contains oxygen and liquid water and can support life.

Earth is the only known planet to support life, and it is the only planet in our solar system not to be named after a Greek or Roman deity.

The first person to set foot on the Moon was astronaut Neil Armstrong.

182

Earth takes 365 days (a year) to rotate once around the Sun. It travels at a speed of 67,000 mph.

The Moon is very hot during the day but very cold at night. The average surface temperature of the Moon is 253°F during the day and –243°F at night.

Soviet Russia successfully landed an unmanned spacecraft on the Moon in 1959, and the USA's Apollo 11 mission in 1969 was the first manned Moon landing.

The Earth's tides are largely caused by the gravitational pull of the Moon.

The Moon is also called Luna and is the Earth's only natural orbiting satellite.

It takes Earth 24 hours (a day) to rotate once on its axis.

Many people think that the shape of the Earth is round or spherical, but its actual shape is an "oblate spheroid." This means it is like a sphere, but the Earth's rotation causes the equator to bulge out in the middle.

Did you know that a person would weigh much less on the Moon? The Moon has much weaker gravity than the Earth due to its smaller mass, so you would weigh about one-sixth of your weight on Earth. That is why lunar astronauts can leap and bound so high in the air.

ROCKY PLANETS

Venus is often called Earth's sister planet because the Earth and Venus are very similar in size with only a 396 mile difference in diameter. Both also have a central core, a molten mantle, and a crust.

Most planets rotate counterclockwise on their axes, but Venus and Uranus rotate clockwise.

Violent storms on Mars can whip up clouds of dust and gas. These can sometimes race round the entire planet, quickly hiding the surface from view. The storms can last for up to a month!

The clouds hiding the solid surface of Venus are full of poisonous gases and acid. Under them, it is hot enough to melt many metals. It is definitely not a place for astronauts to land.

A year on Mercury is much shorter than a year on Earth–it lasts only about 88 Earth days.

None of the terrestrial planets in our solar system have ring systems. Scientists suspect that they may once have had rings, and those rings have disappeared.

To date there have been forty missions to Mars, including orbiters, landers, and rovers. The most recent arrivals include the Mars Curiosity mission in 2012, the MAVEN mission, which arrived on September 22, 2014, followed by the Indian Space Research Organization's MOM Mangalyaan orbiter, which arrived on September 24, 2014.

Thirteen times a century, Mercury passes between the Earth and the Sun in an event called a transit. Mercury appears as a small black dot moving across the face of the Sun. Transits often happen in May or November, and the first observed one was spotted in 1631.

It takes Mars 687 Earth days to orbit the Sun, so a Martian year is nearly twice as long as a year on Earth. Mars also has seasons like ours on Earth.

The smallest terrestrial planet in the solar system is Mercury, which is about a third of the size of Earth. It has a thin atmosphere, which causes it to swing between burning and freezing temperatures.

The surface of Mercury is covered with craters caused by the impact of asteroids and comets. Many of these craters have been named after artists and writers.

Terrestrial planets are Earth-like planets (in Latin, terra means Earth) made up of rocks or metals with a hard surface. Terrestrial planets also have a molten heavy metal core, a few moons, and topological features such as valleys, volcanoes, and craters.

Mercury, Venus, and Mars are the planets nearest Earth. They are all rocky planets and can all be seen with the naked eye from Earth. We have been very successful at sending space probes to find out what they are like.

The brightness of Venus is sometimes mistaken for a UFO. The planet is completely covered by clouds, which makes it extremely reflective to observers looking at the sky on Earth.

Venus not only rotates clockwise, unlike the other planets, but it also rotates very slowly. A day on Venus lasts about 243 Earth days. This means a day on Venus lasts longer than its year, as it takes Venus 225 days to orbit the Sun.

185

THE GIANTS

Jupiter and Saturn are the two giants of the solar system. Both are about ten times bigger than Earth around their middles.

Although they're not as obvious as those of Saturn, Jupiter also has a ring system around its center. It is mostly comprised of dust particles from some of Jupiter's moons caused by impacts from comets and asteroids.

Jupiter has the shortest day of all the planets, as it turns on its axis once every 9 hours and 56 minutes.

The upper atmosphere of Jupiter is divided into cloud belts. They are made primarily of ammonia crystals and sulfur.

Eight spacecraft have visited Jupiter so far–they are Pioneer 10 and 11, Voyager 1 and 2, Galileo, Cassini, Ulysses, and New Horizons. Juno is on its way to Jupiter and will arrive in July 2016.

The first spacecraft to fly by Saturn was Pioneer 11, which launched in 1973 and arrived at Saturn in 1979.

Cassini-Huygens was the first spacecraft to orbit Saturn on July 1, 2004.

Jupiter has 67 confirmed moons in orbit around it. These moons are separated into three groups: Inner, Galilean, and Outer moons. The Inner and Outer moons are the ones closest to and farthest away from Jupiter. The Galilean moons are named after Italian astronomer Galileo Galilei, who discovered them in 1609.

Saturn is 887 million miles from the Sun and takes more than 29 Earth years to orbit the Sun once.

Saturn is easy to spot because of its rings. There are at least seven rings spinning around its middle. The rings are made up of millions of pieces of rock and ice. They stretch out for about 150,000 miles.

Despite its calm appearance, Saturn is not a peaceful planet. Huge storms race around the atmosphere at almost 500 mph.

You could never land on the surface of Jupiter or Saturn because they are not solid. They are huge balls of gas and liquid, with a core of solid rock.

Jupiter is the biggest planet. It is also the heaviest, with a mass two-and-a-half times the mass of all the other planets combined!

Some theories suggest that Jupiter is actually a failed star. Some think that if it had been roughly 80 times more massive, then nuclear fusion would have taken place in the core, and it would have become a star and not a planet.

OUT ON THE EDGE

Uranus and Neptune are the planets farthest from the Sun. They are known as the ice giants. Uranus lies more than 1,740 million miles from the Sun. It is over nineteen times farther from the Sun than Earth is.

There are fourteen moons around Neptune. The most dramatic moon is Triton, a frozen world that spews nitrogen, ice, and dust particles out from below its surface.

Uranus is made of layers of hydrogen, helium, and methane gases. They enclose a layer of water, ammonia, and methane ice. The inner core of the planet is made of rock.

Neptune is smaller than the other ice giant, Uranus. However, despite being smaller in size than Uranus, Neptune has a greater mass.

Uranus is the coldest planet in the solar system, as it emits less heat than it absorbs from the Sun. The temperature on Uranus can dip down to -370 °F.

All twenty-seven moons of Uranus are named after characters from the works of William Shakespeare and Alexander Pope. They include Oberon and Titania, discovered in 1787, and Miranda, discovered in 1948.

Sir William Herschel discovered Uranus in 1781. Initially, Herschel thought it was a comet, but several years later it was confirmed as a planet.

Neptune was the first planet whose existence was mathematically predicted before it was seen through a telescope. It wasn't until 1846 that German astronomer Johann Galle saw the planet for the first time through a telescope.

Neptune is the stormiest planet in our solar system. The winds there can reach speeds of 1,240 mph. That is more than three times the speed of hurricanes on Earth.

The planet Neptune was named after the Roman god of the sea.

Uranus takes 17 hours 14 minutes to complete a rotation, which is almost 7 hours less than Earth's rotation.

Neptune has five very thin rings made of small rocks and dust. They may be formed from what was once one of Neptune's moons.

In 1989, Voyager 2 swept past Neptune and beamed back the first ever close-up images of the Neptune system. This is the only spacecraft that has flown past Neptune.

Methane in Neptune's upper atmosphere absorbs the red light from the Sun and reflects the blue light from the Sun back into space. So when we see the color of Neptune, we are seeing this reflected sunlight with the red color stripped out. This is why Neptune appears blue.

189

A LEAP INTO SPACE

It is only in the last fifty years or so that we have been able to travel into space to see for ourselves what is out there. In that time, we have learned a huge amount.

Since 1962, probes have been sent to all the planets. Some have landed on the planets—on Mars, for example. Others have flown past to collect data and take photographs.

The International Space Station orbits the Earth at about 17,000 mph.

It takes six hours for a space shuttle aboard a crawler-transporter to make the four mile trip from the vehicle assembly building to the launch pad ahead of a space mission.

The International Space Station (ISS) is the biggest object ever flown in space. It has been under construction since its first component was launched in November 1998. Astronauts travel there to live and work for a few months at a time.

Launched on January 31, 1958, *Explorer 1* was the first artificial satellite sent into space by the United States. It orbited Earth every 115 minutes, and its cargo included a cosmic ray detector designed to measure radiation in space.

America's first space station was Skylab, which orbited the Earth from 1973 to 1979. It was longer than a twelve-story building and contained almost 12,000 cubic feet of living space.

The full cost of a spacesuit is about $11 million, although most of this is for the backpack and the control module.

The word "astronaut" comes from the Greek words astron, meaning star, and nautes, which means sailor. The Russian term cosmonaut has a similar root from kosmos, meaning universe.

The ISS is 250 miles above our heads. You can see it in the night sky. It looks like a moving star.

In 1970, Apollo 13 crew members headed to the Moon were met with a dangerous incident when an explosion on board caused serious problems. The astronauts fixed the problems with materials they had on hand and returned home safely.

The spacecraft Voyager 1, launched by NASA in 1977, communicates through radio waves. It left the solar system on August 25, 2012. It is the farthest probe ever launched from Earth and the only to reach interstellar space!

Since 2000, permanent crews have been living and working in space at the International Space Station. There is a permanent crew of three astronauts.

The Mars One mission is part of a project that hopes to send a human crew to land on Mars. However, any volunteers for the mission will have to be prepared for a one-way ticket as there are no plans to return.

Astronauts aboard the ISS see the Sun rise and set every ninety minutes. However, they work 9–5, just like on Earth, to keep their days ordered.

191

HOW FAR CAN WE GO?

Thousands of satellites are sent into space. We use them for communications, weather forecasting, and many other things. Our world would not work without them.

Scientists think that Titan, one of Saturn's moons, is like a young Earth, only much colder. In 2005, a probe landed there and found liquid methane.

A new space telescope to replace Hubble, the James Webb Space Telescope, will be launched in 2018.

Pioneer 10 and Pioneer 11, launched in 1972 and 1973, respectively, were the first spacecraft to visit Jupiter and Saturn.

The Opportunity rover holds the title of longest-running Mars surface mission. It landed on the planet on January 25, 2004 and has been there ever since.

In 2006, Europe's CoRoT spacecraft was launched. It was looking for changes that are happening to stars and new worlds. It studied 120,000 stars before being decommissioned in 2013.

NASA launched its Lunar Crater Observation and Sensing Satellite in June 2009. Its mission was to confirm whether or not there is ice on the Moon. On November 13, 2009, NASA scientists announced the discovery of a "significant amount" of ice in a crater near the Moon's south pole.

NASA's Chandra X-ray Observatory is an observatory in space that scans the skies constantly in X-ray light.

For missions far from the Sun, scientists think that nuclear engines will be needed. With one of these, it might be possible to reach Mars in just a few days!

When NASA's Viking 1 probe touched down on Mars in July 1976, it was the first time a man-made object had landed on the red planet.

The first person in space was 27-year-old Russian cosmonaut Yuri Gagarin. He completed one orbit around the Earth lasting 1 hour 48 minutes on April 12, 1961.

An unmanned spacecraft is currently orbiting Saturn. The spacecraft Cassini-Huygens was launched in 1997 and reached its destination in 2004. It is still there today, studying the planet and its moons, and transmitting data back to Earth.

While in orbit, a space shuttle travels around Earth at a speed of about 17,500 mph.

Phoenix is the successful lander sent to Mars' north pole on August 4, 2007, and it helped scientists to study the ice close to the planet's surface. It even dug the soil and sent the samples to sophisticated chemical analysis instruments. This mission came to an end due to the depletion of solar power as a result of the extreme winter temperatures, and it was concluded on November 10, 2008, after the engineers were unable to contact the lander.

LIVING IN SPACE

The human body is designed to live in Earth's gravity with the presence of oxygen. Because there is no oxygen in outer space, humans cannot survive there without space suits. For humans to live permanently in space, we would need specially adapted environments.

Space adaptation syndrome is a condition that can make astronauts dizzy and sick and is caused by the lack of gravity in space. It is also known as space motion sickness.

One of the major problems of living in the shuttles and stations is the sounds coming from the filters, fans and engines inside the shuttle. These sounds constantly whirr and buzz all around. To overcome this, astronauts often use earplugs.

Sleeping in space is difficult because of the lack of gravity. Astronauts must strap themselves to their bunks to avoid floating around and hitting other objects while they are asleep!

Each space shuttle astronaut is allowed 3.8 lb. of food per day. Foods are individually packaged and stowed for easy handling in space. All food is precooked or processed, so it requires no refrigeration and is either ready to eat or can be prepared simply by adding water or by heating.

Launch and entry space suits are colored orange because this color is easily visible during rescue operations in an emergency. Suits used for spacewalks are white in color to reflect the Sun's heat.

Spacesuits were first invented eighty years ago, initially for pilots who wanted to fly at high altitudes.

The first NASA spacesuits were silver in color because scientists thought this would reflect back the burning hot Sun rays. They had hoses on them that were attached to machines that kept them supplied with air and cooled water.

The average space suit weighs about 310 lb. including the life-support system, and it takes astronauts about forty-five minutes to get into their suits.

Changes in taste play an important role in foods served to the astronauts in space. Some astronauts find that their food is tasteless. A few astronauts enjoy eating certain foods that they would not normally eat, and some experience no change whatsoever.

Astronauts float in space, so they do not use their legs much. This can cause their leg muscles to get weaker and their bones to get thinner. To counteract this, astronauts have to exercise in space every day. They can be strapped to a special treadmill that allows them to walk or jog like on Earth.

It's not just humans who can survive in space—millions of microbes are present there, too. Studies show that a type of bacteria known for causing food-borne illness can change its genetic structure to become more effective after just a few days in space.

Unlike on Earth, as the disks between the vertebrae of the spinal column fail to compress due to the absence of gravity, it will cause the discs to expand, thus making us taller in space!

How do you wash your hair in space? Astronauts do it with a special rinse-free shampoo, originally developed for hospital patients. They wash their bodies with sponges. Only shaving and toothbrushing are performed in the same way as they are on Earth.

The heart works very well in space, but it doesn't have to work as hard as on Earth. Some scientists say that this could lead to a decrease in the size of the heart over the years—this is something that will have to be solved for longer space missions.

CRAZY RECORDS

Ever wondered what the record is for the fastest dog on a skateboard? Or how big the world's largest pizza was? The weird, the wacky, and the wonderful are all collected here—read on at your peril!

09

Dale Moore and Nigel Townsend formed a team to break the record for most martial arts throws in one hour. Together they completed 3,786 judo throws . . . and were very tired after!

The fastest knockout in mixed martial arts history took just seven seconds. Todd Duffee knocked out Tim Hague the moment the bell rang, and his win went down in history.

At just two years old, Dolly Shivani Cherukuri became the youngest Indian citizen to score more than 200 points at an archery trial. And she didn't just break the record, she shattered it, scoring 388 points in total.

The record for deepest underwater cyclist is held by Vittorio Innocente from Italy, who cycled his bike at a depth of 218 ft.

Cyclists Peer Schepanski and Gil Bretschneider hold the record for the highest altitude ever reached by a cyclist. They cycled to 23,658 ft.—only 5,000 ft. lower than the top of Mount Everest! At that height the air contains half the usual amount of oxygen.

Alan Bate of England is the record holder for fastest trip around the world by bike. It took him 125 days, 21 hours, and 45 minutes to bike 18,310.47 miles.

Australian cyclist Andrew Hellinga holds the world record for cycling backwards. He made it just over 209 miles—that's a four-hour drive in a car!

The highest-earning tennis player in the world is Roger Federer, with $94 million in earnings over his career so far. Not a sporting achievement, but a crazy amount of money!

College wrestler Cael Sanderson has won the most National Collegiate wrestling matches ever—159 in total.

Not only has Aneta Florczyk of Poland won the World's Strongest Woman four times, she also holds the strange record of Most People Lifted and Thrown in Two Minutes. Florczyk threw twelve!

The oldest competing gymnast in the world is Johanna Quaas. She can still perform cartwheels at 87 years old.

Boxer Rocky Marciano holds the longest unbroken winning streak in boxing history. Not only did he win the title of Heavyweight Champion of the World, but his professional career saw him win forty-nine fights in a row. And forty-three of those he won by knock-out!

Australian tennis player Samuel Groth holds the record for fastest serve of a tennis ball. He clocked in a speed of 163.4 mph. That's faster than the fastest baseball pitch (105 mph) and the fastest soccer shot (114 mph).

Tennis ace Martina Navratilova holds the record for winning the Wimbledon Championships six times in a row. No other woman has won more than three times in a row, so her record is very safe.

The longest tennis match in history happened at the 2010 Wimbledon Championship and went on for eleven hours and five minutes. The match was between John Isner (USA) and Nicolas Mahut (France).

TEAM SPORTS

The National League of Professional Baseball Clubs is the oldest sports league in America. It was founded in 1876.

Baseball Hall of Famer Luis Aparicio holds the record for most games in one position. He played shortstop for all 2,581 games of his major league career.

In 1957 baseball player Richie Ashburn broke a spectator's nose when he fouled a ball. A few minutes later he fouled another ball, and it hit the same woman as she was being stretchered out!

Rugby was invented in England. It is similar to American football, but the players don't wear protective equipment. The largest rugby scrum of all time took place in Australia in 2015, with 1,160 people taking part.

Although baseball is America's national sport, Cuba has won the Baseball World Cup a record twenty-five times, while America has only won it four times.

The longest losing streak in American football history goes to the Tampa Bay Buccaneers. They lost 26 games in a row. And when the Buccaneers finally won a game, the coach for the opposing team was instantly fired.

American football is the most dangerous sport in the world. There are an estimated 1.2 million football-related injuries per year.

Brazilian soccer player Pelé scored an amazing 127 goals in just one year. The closest anyone else has gotten is 91 goals in a year, 40 percent less than Pelé's record.

The world record for the longest basketball shot is 415 ft. Brett Stanford of the How Ridiculous trick shot team took the shot from the top of the Gordon River Dam in Tasmania, Australia.

The lowest trade price in ice hockey history goes to Kris Draper, who was traded for just $1 to the Detroit Red Wings. He got the nickname "One Dollar Man" but went on to win four Stanley Cups with Detroit.

The oldest ice hockey player in the world is Johannes Loos. On December 19, 2014, Loos played for the Huff 'N Puff Hockey League in London, Ontario, Canada. He was 85 years and 1 day old.

In cricket, whoever scores the most runs wins. They run between two points called wickets. Sachin Tendulkar from India has the record for most runs. He scored 15,921 test match runs in his twenty-four year career. That's almost 200 miles!

Taking a wicket in cricket is when you bowl the ball and it knocks over the wicket behind the batsman and puts him out of the game. Wilfred Rhodes has taken 4,204 wickets in First-class matches, the most of any cricketer. That's good aim!

The most popular sport in the world is soccer, with 3.5 billion fans worldwide. That's more than a third of the people on the planet.

Cricket is the second most popular sport in the world, with 2.5 billion fans. Field hockey comes in third with 2 billion fans.

ATHLETICS

A marathon is a long-distance run of 26 miles and 385 yd. The fastest man to run a marathon is Dennis Kimetto of Kenya. He finished in two hours, two minutes and fifty-seven seconds. The fastest woman is Britain's Paula Radcliffe, who finished in two hours, fifteen minutes and twenty-five seconds.

The record for the most marathons run in a single year is held by Rob Young from Britain. He ran 370 marathons in 365 days—that's more than one a day! That is the equivalent of running from London to Australia.

The most world records set by an individual in athletics is thirty-five. Sergey Bubka of Ukraine was a pole vaulter who set seventeen outdoor and eighteen indoor records between 1984 and 1994. He is still the current record-holder in both.

The fastest man in the world is the Jamaican sprinter Usain Bolt. Bolt is the first man to hold the world record for both the 100 and 200 meter sprints since modern time-keeping began.

Uwe Hohn became the first person to throw the javelin over 100 meters. It was a very windy day, and that helped carry the javelin to 104.80 meters. After his throw the javelin was redesigned so the wind had less effect on it.

American athlete Florence Griffith Joyner set the world record for fastest women's 100 meter sprint way back in 1988. She ran it in 10.49 seconds, and nobody has come close ever since!

The record for fastest backwards run over a mile is just 6:02.35 minutes. It was set by D. Joseph James of India in 2002.

The first medal given out at the modern Olympics, held in Athens in 1896, was to American triple jumper James Connolly. At the time, the top medal was made of silver, not gold.

Despite having a population of just 3 million people, compared with the USA's 318 million, Jamaica has won seventeen Olympic gold medals, most of them for sprinting.

Wheelchair racing is a Paralympic sport for disabled athletes. The current record holder for the 100 meter race is David Brown of the USA, who raced to victory in just 10.92 seconds.

The oldest track-and-field record has been standing for so long that the country the runner was from no longer exists! Jarmila Kratochvílová of Czechoslovakia ran the 800 meter race in one minute, fifty-three seconds.

The longest wheelie in a wheelchair was performed by Xie Junwu of China, who stayed on two wheels for 16.03 miles.

A decathlon is an athletics event combining ten track and field events: four runs, three jumps, and three throws. The world record holders for men and women are Ashton Eaton (USA) with 9,045 points and Austra Skujytė (Lithuania) with 8,366 points.

WATER SPORTS

The first person to swim across the English Channel without a life jacket was Englishman Matthew Webb. The crossing is twenty-one miles, but Webb swam a total of thirty-eight miles to make it from Dover, England, to Calais, France, in twenty-one hours forty-five minutes.

In 1926 Gertrude Ederle became the first woman to swim the English Channel. She crossed in just fourteen hours and thirty-one minutes and was only nineteen years old.

The largest swimming lesson ever given in a single venue took place in Naples, Florida, in 2014. The event was attended by 1,308 people at the Sun-N-Fun Lagoon.

The farthest anyone has surfed on a single wave is 43.1 miles. Gary Saavedra from Panama set the record surfing on the Panama Canal. He followed a wave-creating boat and surfed for just under four hours.

The longest journey swimming is 3,273.38 miles. It was set by Martin Strel of Slovenia, who swam the whole length of the Amazon River. It took him just over two months to complete the journey.

The most gold medals won at a single Olympic Games is held by swimmer Michael Phelps of the USA. He won eight golds at the 2008 Beijing Olympics.

Half of the USA's world swimming records are held by just two men: Michael Phelps holds seven and Ryan Lochte holds five.

The United States leads the planet in swimming world records. The country's swimmers have set and hold twenty-four records in total. That's more than three times as many as the second-place country, Germany, with seven records set.

The longest distance sailed in twenty-four hours is 908.2 nautical miles. The record was set in a trimaran called Banque Populaire V and was made during the fastest crossing of the Atlantic.

The oldest person to sail around the world on their own and non-stop was Minoru Saito from Japan. He was seventy-two years old, and the journey took him 233 days to complete.

The largest sailing race on a single day was Bart's Bash in 2014. A total of 9,484 boats took part at 237 locations around the world.

The fastest anyone has sailed around the world solo is just fifty-seven days, thirteen hours, thirty-four minutes, and six seconds! The record was set by Francis Joyon from France in 2008.

There are a few contenders for the record of world's highest dive. Although some have dived farther, the only diver to make it over 170 ft. without injury is Dana Kunze of San Diego, California, who dived 172 ft. in 1983.

A free dive is when a diver swims as far down as they can just holding their breath. The record for the deepest free dive is held by Croatian diver Goran Čolak, who got 896 ft. under water. That's almost three football fields!

Diving is one of the most popular Olympic sports with spectators. The first diving board was set up in Hampstead Ponds in London so that gymnasts could practice their tumbles without landing on the hard ground.

MOTORSPORTS

A pit stop is when a vehicle stops during a race to refuel, replace the tires, and make repairs. Pit stops have to be very quick to get the driver back in the race. The fastest pit stop ever was 1.923 seconds long, completed by the Red Bull Racing team.

The world's first racetrack was called Brooklands. It was built in Weybridge, England, in 1907 and was also one of Britain's first airfields. Today it is part of a museum for vintage automobiles.

Stock car racing uses ordinary cars that have been strengthened so they can collide with each other. NASCAR is the world's largest governing body for stock car racing.

The most popular motorsport in the world is Formula One. Competitors drive solo in super-fast cars and compete in a series of races known as Grands Prix to win the Formula One championship.

Indy Car racing is the most popular motorsport in America. The main difference between Formula One and Indy Car is that Indy Car racers all use the same type of car, while in Formula One different types of car are allowed.

Robbie Maddison is an Australian motorbike stunt rider known for setting crazy records. He holds the record for longest trick on a bike when he performed a Superman Seat Grab (it looks how it sounds) over a 246-ft. jump.

The record for the most cars taking part in a race was 216. The race took place on September 13, 2014, and was held to raise money for a children's cancer charity.

The fastest robot on a motorbike is Yamaha-designed Motobot. Its current top speed is 65 mph, but technology is being developed that will allow it to top 124 mph.

German driver Michael Schumacher holds the record for most Formula One wins. He won ninety-one races, almost double the second place driver, Alain Prost, who won fifty-one races.

GRAND PRIX CHAMPION

Retired NASCAR driver Richard Petty holds the record for most NASCAR wins. He has won 200 races. His nearest challenger has only won 105, so it'll be a while before anyone catches up to this speed demon.

SPEED

Supersonic speeds are faster than the speed of sound (340.29 miles per second). They are measured in Machs. Mach 1 is the speed of sound, Mach 2 is twice the speed of sound, and so on. NASA's X-43A scramjet can travel at Mach 9.6—that's nearly 7,000 mph—making it the fastest jet in the world.

The fastest fish is the sailfish. It can swim as fast as a cheetah can run—70 mph. If it were on land, it could outrace a car!

The fastest electric aircraft that can carry a person is the E-Crystaline. It can fly at 163 mph and is powered by lithium batteries.

The fastest computer in the world is the Tianhe-2, built by the Chinese firm Inspur and China's National University of Defense Technology in Guangzhou, China.

The fastest passenger train is the L0 Series, a Japanese train that reaches 375 mph.

The land speed record is the highest speed a person can go on the land in any vehicle. The current record is 763.035 mph, and is held by Andy Green of Britain.

The official air speed record for a manned air-breathing jet aircraft is held by the Lockheed SR-71 Blackbird, with a speed of 2,193 mph.

The Westland Lynx is a British military helicopter that can travel at 249 mph, making it the fastest helicopter in the world.

The fastest thing in the universe is light. It travels at 186,282.397 miles per second! That means it can go around the world over 7.4 times in one second.

The peregrine falcon is a bird of prey about the size of a crow. When it dives to catch its prey—usually smaller birds or mammals—it can reach speeds of 200 mph, making it not only the fastest bird but the fastest animal in the world.

The fastest land animal in the world is the cheetah, a large cat that lives in Africa and parts of Iran. It can run at speeds up to 70 mph.

209

SCARY STUNTS

Fearless tightrope walker Freddy Nock set the world record for highest tightrope walk in 2015. He walked between two mountaintops in the Swiss Alps at over 3,000 ft.

Human cannonball David Smith Jr. holds the record for farthest distance for a human shot from a cannon. He reached 193 ft. 8.8 in. in March 2011 and traveled at 74.56 mph.

Annie Edson Taylor was the first person to successfully go over Niagara Falls and live to tell the tale. In 1901 she hopped inside a wooden barrel and plunged 173 ft., coming out with only a cut on her forehead.

Eustace wasn't much of a daredevil before he completed his super high jump in 2014. He was a computer scientist who used to work for Google.

American Alan Eustace holds the world record for highest free-fall skydive. He jumped from 25.7 miles above the Earth . . . that's from space! And it's over four times the height of Mount Everest.

Jackie Chan shot to fame for performing daredevil stunts in his movies. He has crawled across hot coals, hung onto a speeding bus using only an umbrella, and fallen off a clock tower with only a few awnings to break his fall.

The Human Spider, Alain Robert of France, has climbed the Eiffel Tower, the Sydney Opera House, and the Petronas Twin Towers, all without any safety line or permission—he was arrested at the top of every one!

A BASE jump is when you skydive from the top of a building or other fixed structure, like a cliff. It's much more dangerous than skydiving from a plane and is banned in some countries.

The highest BASE jump was from the tallest building in the world, the Burj Khalifa tower in Dubai. It was set by Fred Fugen and Vince Reffet, both from France.

Evel Knievel was a famous motorcycle stunt-rider who jumped rows of trucks, cars, and even sharks on his motorcycle. He holds the record for most broken bones in a lifetime, suffering 433 bone fractures. Ouch!

A dog called Whisper became the world's first BASE jumping dog in 2014. He was owned by Dean Potter, a famous climber and BASE jumper.

Some BASE jumps are performed in wingsuits, which have fabric stretched between the legs and under the arms to increase the surface area of the body and make it possible to glide like a flying squirrel.

One of the first world-famous daredevils was magician Harry Houdini. In the early 1900s, Houdini performed many daring escapes, including being buried alive and locked and handcuffed inside a tank of water.

Famous daredevil Eddie Kidd performed over 3,000 death-defying motorcycle jumps, including one over the Great Wall of China and another over a 50-ft. tall viaduct.

MUSIC

The longest music video of all time is "Happy" by Pharrell Williams. It lasts twenty-four hours and features people dancing and lip-syncing to the song, which is played on a loop over 360 times.

Thrash metal group Metallica was the first musical group to play a concert on every continent of the world, even Antarctica, where they performed for 120 scientists.

The oldest musical instruments in the world are flutes made of bone. They were found in Germany and are believed to be 42,000 to 43,000 years old. They are carved from bird bones and mammoth ivory.

The world's highest paid musician is Dr. Dre, who took home $620 million in 2014. Most of that was made through his business selling headphones.

The record for fastest selling album on iTunes belongs to Beyoncé, whose fifth album, also named Beyoncé, sold 828,773 copies worldwide in three days in December 2013.

The largest electric guitar in the world is 43 ft. 7.5 in. long, 16 ft. 5.5 in. wide, and weighs 2,000 lb. Despite its huge size, it's still possible to play it!

The most expensive musical instrument in the world was a violin that sold at auction for $15,875,800. It was a Stradivarius violin, made by the Stradivari family in the seventeenth century.

The most people to play a piano at the same time is eighteen. Music teacher Angela Montemurro and seventeen of her students played a piece of music called "Galop Marche" by Albert Lavignac.

The classical composer Haydn has two skulls in his tomb. His head was stolen after he died, so it was replaced with another skull. Then the original skull was found and put in the tomb too!

The classical composer Franz Liszt got so many requests from fans asking for a lock of his hair that he bought a dog and sent fur clippings instead.

Composer John Cage wrote a piece of music called "As Slow As Possible." It is being played right now and will last 639 years.

The world's fastest rapper is NoClue who can rap 14.1 syllables per second.

Thriller won Michael Jackson eight Grammy awards in 1984, the most Grammys won by an artist in a single night.

The most expensive opera costume of all time cost over $23 million. It was worn by singer Adelina Patti at Covent Garden Opera House in 1895.

The best-selling album of all time is Thriller by Michael Jackson. It has sold over 65 million copies across the world.

213

MOVIES & TELEVISION

The smallest stop-motion film ever is "A Boy and his Atom" made by computer company IBM. It measures just 45 by 25 nanometers—that's 45 x 25 billionths of a meter! The pixels are made of single molecules of carbon monoxide.

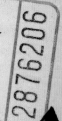

2876206

The record for most movies seen in one year is 1,132. Maggie Correa-Avilés set the record in 2010 and watched most of the films alongside her dog, Morgana.

Hong Kong actor Jackie Chan holds the world record for most stunts by a living actor. He has appeared in more than one hundred films and has performed stunts in all of them!

Jackie Chan also holds the record for most credits on a single film. For his film *Chinese Zodiac* he had fifteen credits, including writer, director, actor, producer, executive producer, stuntman, and even theme-tune vocalist.

Academy Awards are given out for achievements in film. Three movies hold the record for winning the most awards, known as Oscars: *Ben Hur* (1959), *Titanic* (1997), and *The Lord of the Rings: The Return of the King* (2003) all won eleven awards.

When a movie director doesn't want anyone to know he or she made a film, the name Allen (or Alan) Smithee is used instead of his or her own name. The first film to have the director listed as Alan Smithee was *Death of a Gunfighter*.

In 2015, dinosaur epic *Jurassic World* had the biggest opening weekend of any movie. It made $524,418,134 worldwide in just a few days!

The film *Swearnet* holds the record for most swears in a feature film. In total the cast swears 935 times . . . leaving very little room for a plot.

The oldest open-air cinema still operating is the Sun Picture Theatre in Broome, Western Australia, which opened in 1916. Moviegoers sit on folding chairs on the beach.

Movie extras are people in the background of scenes who don't have lines. The movie that used the most extras in a single scene was *Gandhi*, which told the story of Mahatma Gandhi, leader of the Indian independence movement. A total of 300,000 extras were used in the scene depicting his funeral.

The most paid to a single screenwriter for the script to a movie was $4 million. It was paid to Shane Black for his script *The Long Kiss Goodnight*. $5 million was shared by Terry Rossio and Bill Marsilii for their script *Déjà Vu*.

The youngest film director to make a professional feature-length film is Saugat Bista from Nepal. He was only 7 years and 340 days old when *Love You Baba* was released in theaters.

Pirates of the Caribbean: On Stranger Tides is the most expensive movie ever made. It cost $378.5 million. The second most expensive is *Pirates of the Caribbean: At World's End*, which cost $300 million. Both made over three times more than their budget.

Bollywood in India is the world's largest movie industry. Bollywood produces over 800 movies per year, while Hollywood produces around 400 movies.

Detective character Sherlock Holmes is the most portrayed literary human character in film and television. He has been depicted 254 times, and the number is growing all the time.

28762O6

LITERATURE

The smallest book in the world is a copy of *Teeny Ted from Turnip Town*, by Robert Chaplin. It measures a tiny 70 micrometers by 100 micrometers and is so small it has to be read with an electron microscope.

The most books signed by one author in a single session is 4,649 by Chinese writer Sammy Lee. Her novel was called *Autopilot Leadership Model*.

The longest memoir ever written was 3,600 pages long. It was written by Giacomo Casanova, an Italian adventurer who was famous for having many romantic affairs.

The Nobel Prize for Literature is the literary award with the biggest prize money. Winners receive 8 million Swedish kronor, or $1,142,000.

The longest novel ever published is *In Search of Lost Time* by French novelist Marcel Proust. It is about memories that appear in our minds from nowhere.

The youngest published author was Dorothy Straight of Washington, D.C., who wrote *How the World Began* in 1962 at age four.

The best-selling author of all time is English playwright William Shakespeare. An estimated 4 billion of his plays and poetry collections have been sold worldwide.

The first use of the word "book" is in a book written by Alfred the Great, who was King of Wessex in England.

The Dewey Decimal System is a system for categorizing books. The writer Isaac Asimov (1920–1992) is the only author to have published a book in nine out of the ten Dewey library categories.

The best-selling fiction novel of all time is *A Tale of Two Cities* by Charles Dickens. It was published in 1859 and had sold over 200 million copies. It is set in London and Paris during the French Revolution.

The oldest book ever found is thought to be the Etruscan gold book. It dates to around 660 BCE, making it over 2,500 years old. The book is made from six sheets of 24-carat gold held together by rings.

One in five adults in the world cannot read or write.

People in India read the most, spending on average 10.7 hours a week reading.

The oldest bound book is the Nag Hammadi library. The pages are made from papyrus (a type of grass), and it has a leather cover. It was found buried in a jar in Egypt and is thought to be 1,693 years old.

Part of the M6 motorway (freeway) in the UK was built on books. An amazing 2.5 million copies of pulped novels were used in its construction.

FOOD

The most expensive edible fungus in the world is the white truffle. It costs $1,500 per pound and is found only in a few places in Italy, Slovenia, and France.

The world's most dangerous food is the puffer fish. It is full of poison that can kill you, and only a small part is safe to eat. Chefs train for many years to learn how to cut it correctly.

The most expensive coffee in the world is made of poop! Civet coffee is made of partly-digested coffee cherries that have been eaten and pooped out by an animal called a civet. It costs between $100 and $600 per pound.

The most expensive food in the world is beluga caviar. It's the eggs of the beluga sturgeon fish and costs from $3,200 to $4,500 per pound.

Chocolate was so popular with the Aztec people, who lived in Mexico in the fourteenth century, that they accepted it from the Mayan people as a form of currency, like gold.

The world's most expensive herb is saffron. It's made from part of a crocus flower and is used to flavor and color food. A single ounce of the best quality saffron costs $8.29.

The spicy heat of a chili is measured in units called Scovilles. A jalapeño pepper measures 1,000 to 4,000 on the Scoville scale. The hottest chili in the world, the Carolina Reaper, measures 1,600,000 to 2,200,000! People have fainted after tasting it.

The first soup ever made was created in 6,000 BCE. It was made of hippopotamus and sparrows!

A samosa is a delicious fried pastry made across Asia. The largest samosa ever made was a massive 244 lb. 4 oz. It was made at Bradford College in the UK and measured 53 in. long and 33 in. wide.

The world's largest omelet weighed over seven tons and was made with a total of 880 lb. of oil and 145,000 eggs. The massive meal was made in the town of Ferreira do Zêzere in Portugal.

The longest pizza ever was made in Italy in 2015 and was nearly one mile long. It contained 1.5 tons of mozzarella cheese, 330 lb. of olive oil, and 2 tons of tomato sauce. It took eighteen hours and five ovens to bake the pizza!

The world's largest burger weighs 134 lb. and comes in a bun that weighs 50 lb.!

One fast food hamburger can contain the meat from 100 different cows!

The largest bubble gum bubble ever blown measured 20 in. across. The record is held by Chad Fell of Alabama.

ANIMALS

Is it a bird? Is it a plane? No, it's a dog on a skateboard! Jumpy the dog set the record for fastest 100 meters on a skateboard in 2013 when he completed it in 19.65 seconds.

Tigger, a dog owned by Bryan and Christina Flessner, has the longest ears, measuring 12.25 in. and 13.5 in. for the right and left ears, respectively.

The smallest donkey in the world lives at Best Friends Farm in Gainesville, Florida. KneeHi, who was born in October 2007, stands just 25.29 in. tall—as his name suggests, that's about knee-high.

The farthest a cat has ever jumped—and been recorded—is 6 ft. The cat is called Alley and is owned by American Samantha Martin.

The tallest dog in the world was almost twice the height of the smallest donkey. Zeus the Great Dane measured 44 in. tall, and when standing on his hind legs, he was over 7 ft. tall!

The dog with the loudest bark in the world is a golden retriever called Charlie. His bark is almost as loud as a rock concert at 113.1 decibels.

The smallest dog in the world is a chihuahua called Milly. She is only 3.8 in. tall, can fit in the palm of your hand, and is about as big as an adult man's sneaker.

The blue whale is the largest living animal on the planet. It can measure from 75—100 ft. and weighs as much as 150 tons. That's as long as a ten-story building!

The two biggest bunnies in the world are father and son. Darius is the biggest. He measures 4 ft. 4 in. and weighs 49 lb. His son Jeff measures 3 ft. 8 in. and is still growing!

The fluffiest bunny in the world is an Angora rabbit called Franchesca. Her fur measures 14.37 in.—that's longer than a foot-long sandwich!

The world's most deadly animal is the mosquito, which carries a host of diseases, including malaria. Diseases resulting from mosquito bites kill 2 to 3 million people every year.

The world's highest-ranking law enforcement camel is Bert, who is Reserve Deputy Sheriff for the Los Angeles County Sheriff's Department, San Dimas.

The oldest animal ever discovered was a quahog clam discovered off the coast of Iceland in 2006. The clam was between 405 and 410 years old.

The longest snake living in captivity is Medusa the reticulated python, who lives in Kansas City, Missouri. She measures 25 ft. 2 in. long and has eaten a whole deer all at once!

The bird with the largest egg is the ostrich. The biggest ostrich egg ever found weighed a massive 11.36 ounces.

221

RANDOM RECORDS

American Brad Byers holds the record for "The Most Swords Swallowed and Twisted at One Time." He swallowed twelve 27.5-inch swords and then twisted all twelve swords 180 degrees in his throat.

In 2014, 4,483 people in Bangkok, Thailand, hula-hooped for seven minutes to set the world record for the most people simultaneously hula-hooping.

In 2013, Serbian Dalibor Jablanović set the record for most spoons balanced on a face. He managed to balance thirty-one spoons.

The world's largest pocket knife measured 12.8 ft. and weighed 48.5 lb. Telmo Cadavez from Portugal designed the knife.

Spoons are a popular tool for record breakers. Etibar Elchiyev of Azerbaijan holds the record for most spoons on a human body. He had fifty-three metal spoons magnetized to his neck and chest.

The most tattooed man in the world is Lucky Diamond Rich. He is a chainsaw juggler, unicycler, and sword-swallower who has spent over 1,000 hours being tattooed.

Nobody knows where he got the idea, but Tafzi Ahmed of Germany set and holds the world record for smashing watermelons with his head. Ahmed smashed forty-three watermelons in one minute to set the record.

The craziest juggling record has to go to Milan Roskopf of Slovakia, who juggled three dangerous chainsaws 62 times in a row!

Kazuhiro Watanabe, a fashion designer from Japan, holds the world record for the tallest Mohawk. Watanabe's hair stands at 3 ft. 8.6 in.

The world record for most world records held by one person is Ashrita Furman, who has dedicated his life to breaking world records. He has set 236 world records, and the most he has held at one time is 100.

One of Ashrita Furman's oddest records is most eggs crushed with his head in one minute. He crushed eighty eggs.

Chris Walton, known as "The Duchess," has the longest fingernails in the world. She has been growing them for eighteen years, and they measure 10 ft. 2 in. on her left hand and 9 ft. 7 in. on her right hand.

Ted Batchelor of California holds the record for longest distance run while on fire! He ran 529 ft. and 10 in. while performing what's known as a full-body-burn. To do it Ted wore a special suit that stops him from getting burned.

Most people couldn't eat one super-hot Bhut Jolokia chili pepper. Jason McNabb of California ate 2.33 ounces of the fearsomely hot peppers in just two minutes to claim his world record.

Most of us run when we see a bee, but beekeeper She Ping from China loves his bees so much he covered his body in them for the world record. He was covered in 73 lb. of bees!

Picture Credits
All images © iStock / Getty Images